S0-FBM-816

OUTLINES
OF METAPHYSICS

BY

JOHN S. MACKENZIE

M.A. Glasg., Litt.D. Camb.

PROFESSOR OF LOGIC AND PHILOSOPHY IN THE UNIVERSITY COLLEGE OF SOUTH
WALES AND MONMOUTHSHIRE ; FORMERLY FELLOW OF TRINITY COLLEGE,
CAMBRIDGE ; AUTHOR OF 'AN INTRODUCTION TO SOCIAL PHILOSOPHY'
AND 'A MANUAL OF ETHICS'

SECOND EDITION REVISED

London
MACMILLAN AND CO., LIMITED
NEW YORK : THE MACMILLAN COMPANY
1906

First Edition, 1902.
Second Edition, 1906.

GLASGOW: PRINTED AT THE UNIVERSITY PRESS BY
ROBERT MACLEHOSE AND CO. LTD.

PREFACE

THE publication of so small a book, dealing with so vast a subject, certainly calls for some explanation. It is the outcome of a larger plan—the *ridiculus mus*, as some may think, that has issued from a too ambitious undertaking. I had promised a good many years ago to write a book for Sonnenschein's Library of Philosophy, giving a comprehensive and connected survey of philosophical first principles, as these appear in the light of the most recent developments of thought. This promise may at some time be fulfilled; but the duties of a teacher of Philosophy in a provincial College are not favourable to large constructive efforts; and several circumstances have made this particular attempt appear less urgent than it once did. The publication of Mr. Bradley's great work on *Appearance and Reality* might well give pause to any one who had a similar design in view. If his brilliant dialectic and subtle speculative insight had failed to produce a convincing scheme of philosophic truth, the prospect was not very encouraging for the smaller fry. On the other hand, so far as he had succeeded, further attempts in the same direction became unnecessary

It was partly for this reason, as well as for the other that I have indicated, that I decided, for a time at least, to abandon the larger scheme, and attempt something smaller and more feasible. It seemed to me that a short introductory book might at least be of some use in helping students to a more easy understanding of the larger ones—a book that should aim chiefly at indicating the place and nature of the various metaphysical problems, rather than at thrashing them out in detail. The difficulty of metaphysical study lies largely, I think, in the bewildering way in which one problem rises out of another, like hills appearing over one another's crests. The mere attempt to put them in some sort of order may have a certain value. Of course a book that attempts to do little more than this cannot be of much use to the philosophical investigator, who aims at thinking out some special problem. Nor can it be expected to have any great attraction for the general reader who is interested in philosophical inquiries. Such a reader will usually desire to find solutions of difficulties, rather than indications of the points at which they lie and slight suggestions of methods by which they may be dealt with. Such a book as I refer to would be chiefly serviceable to the student who is just beginning seriously to face the great issues that are included under the term Metaphysics. A student at this stage is apt to lose his way, and often to lose heart at the same time, in the midst of a multitude of disconnected problems, and of divergent systems that seek by various methods to deal with them. The histories of Philosophy do not wholly remove this difficulty; and even the Introductions to Philosophy, that have become so numerous in recent years, do not appear —partly, perhaps, because they are most often of foreign extraction—to meet the needs of the ordinary English reader. It seemed to to me that, in view of the recent constructive work that has been attempted in our own country, it ought now to be possible, in a quite short sketch, to give enough indication of the nature of the problems to enable the student to find his bearings among them. This is what I have here tried to do.

The chief difficulty of such an attempt lies in the necessity of combining two requirements that appear almost incompatible with one another. A text-book that is to be of any real value to the student must be alive. To point to the various problems as if they were speci- mens in a museum, would obviously be to fail entirely in the object that is aimed at — viz., that of bringing out the vital relationships of the various points that have to be considered. On the other hand, a text-book of this kind must not aim at superseding, in the minds of those who use it, the works to which it is an intro- duction. I have kept both these points steadily in view; but I can hardly hope that I have been completely successful in avoiding the dangers to which I refer. My aim at least has been to produce a book which is a living unity within itself, and which yet points continu- ally outwards to the larger life of the speculative thought of the world.

The general method of treatment that I have adopted is genetic. The application of this method to Philosophy was partly suggested by the study of Aristotle and Hegel, partly by some papers in *Mind* by Professor Dewey, and perhaps most of all by some hints that I got in lecture and conversation from Mr. G. F. Stout, when I was an undergraduate in Cambridge.[1] I am more and more convinced that we cannot hope to understand any living thing except by considering how it grows; and I am also more and more convinced that nothing is more truly alive than human thought.

Mr. Stout has kindly read this little book through in manuscript. I feel that I owe a great deal to his penetrating criticisms, and perhaps quite as much to his sympathetic appreciation and encouragement.

CARDIFF,
January, 1902.

---

[1] A book was published a few years ago entitled *Genetic Philosophy* by Mr. D. J. Hill; but I do not think that his method has much in common with mine.

CONTENTS.

CHAPTER IV.

THE METHODS OF METAPHYSICS.

BOOK II.   THE GENESIS OF EXPERIENCE.

CHAPTER I.

THE GENERAL NATURE OF CONSCIOUS GROWTH.

CHAPTER II.

SENSATION.

CHAPTER III.

PERCEPTION.

CHAPTER IV.

THOUGHT.

CHAPTER V.

RESULTS OF THE GENETIC SURVEY.

BOOK III. CRITICISM OF IDEAL CONSTRUCTIONS.

CHAPTER I.

PERCEPTUAL CONSTRUCTION.

CHAPTER II.

SCIENTIFIC CONSTRUCTION.

CHAPTER III.

ETHICAL CONSTRUCTION.

CHAPTER IV.

AESTHETIC CONSTRUCTION.

CHAPTER V.

RELIGIOUS CONSTRUCTION.

CHAPTER VI.

SPECULATIVE CONSTRUCTION.

CHAPTER VII.

OUTLINES OF METAPHYSICS

BOOK I. INTRODUCTION.

CHAPTER I.

THE PROBLEM OF METAPHYSICS.

1. Definition of Metaphysics. Metaphysics[1] may be provisionally defined as the science that seeks to deal with experience as a whole, or rather as a systematic unity. What exactly this means, will, it is hoped, become more apparent as we proceed. The term Philosophy is often used in a sense practically equivalent to Metaphysics, but is somewhat less precise in its application, and is generally understood as including some subsidiary and closely related subjects.[2] With this preliminary understanding of the

---

[1] The word itself has a quite accidental origin, referring simply to the writings of Aristotle that came after those dealing with Physics. But it has clung to the subject, mainly, I suppose, on account of the suggestion that it conveys of principles that underlie those used in physical inquiries. Some remarks on the original meaning of the term will be found in the article on Metaphysic by Dr. Edward Caird in the *Encyclopaedia Britannica*, to which I may take this opportunity of giving a general reference. It is reprinted in his *Essays on Literature and Philosophy*, Vol. II.

[2] Philosophy used to be regarded as including Natural and Moral Philosophy. The former is now known as Physics. Philosophy is

subject-matter of our study, we may readily see how it is distinguished from those special sciences that deal with some part or aspect of experience. But the distinction may be made clearer by noticing some of the different types of such sciences.

(*a*) Geology may be taken as a good type of what is understood by a special science. Here the subject-matter is obviously a limited one, and it is quite easy to point to parts of our experience with which the science has no concern. The experience of pain, for instance, and everything else that we commonly describe as purely subjective, lie outside its province; and so do the general facts of life, though on some facts of life it may indirectly throw light. Other parts of our experience, again, though not so entirely excluded by it, are yet not directly dealt with by it. Numbers, for instance, will almost inevitably be used by the geologist in his investigations, but it is no part of his business to consider the nature and relations of numbers as such. Similarly, though all the facts with which he is concerned are in space, and all the processes with which he deals take place in time. yet, simply as a geologist, he has nothing to do with the nature of space and time. Nor is it even his business to inquire into the ultimate chemical composition of the substances with which he deals, or into the ultimate nature of the forces by which their changes are determined, or into the ultimate laws by which the movements of their parts are governed. Such

---

at present generally understood as including Logic, Psychology, Ethics, Metaphysics, Aesthetics, and the general theory of Society and the State. The theory of Education is also commonly treated as a closely related subject. Reference may be made to the article on Philosophy by Professor A. Seth in the *Encyclopaedia Britannica*.

inquiries he leaves to Chemistry or Physics or Mechanics, though it may be necessary for him, in the prosecution of his own researches, to assume the truth of the results of these other sciences and possibly to discover facts that may lead to the modification of some of them. In such a case as this, then, we can readily see that the science is limited to a part of experience; and that even that part is regarded only in some particular aspects.

(*b*) If we take Biology, again, as our instance, it is equally easy to see that its province is a limited one. The fundamental questions referred to in connection with Geology, such as those of number, space, time, composition, force, motion, etc., are equally beyond the province of Biology. Again, it is easy to point to special facts, such as the existence of iron or sulphuric acid or other inorganic conditions, with which Biology has no direct concern. There is, however, one important point in which it seems to differ from Geology in its general character as a science, viz., that it raises an ultimate problem which it does not appear to be able to pass on to any other science. All the ultimate questions involved in the subject-matter of Geology seem to be relegated, for their final answer, to Chemistry, Physics, and other special sciences, except such questions as those about the general nature of space and time, with respect to which it may at least be said that they concern other sciences quite as much as they concern Geology. In the case of Biology, on the other hand, the question as to the general nature of life presents itself as an ultimate problem; and it seems to be a problem that belongs particularly to this scienee, and cannot be passed on to any other. And if Biology were to set itself resolutely to deal with this problem, facing all the issues that are contained in it, it would probably find itself involved in the whole question with regard to the nature of our experience and of the world that is presented to us in it. The often quoted saying of Tennyson about the flower is probably rigorously true :

> " If I could understand
> What you are, root and all and all in all,
> I should know what God and Man is."

But in reality Biology, as commonly understood, does not definitely deal with this ultimate question at all. In fact, the tendency at present seems to be to split up Biology itself into the two independent sciences of Zoology and Botany, and thus to leave us with no general science of life at all. This point, however, brings us a little nearer to an understanding of the kind of problem that is left over for Metaphysics. The place of life in our general experience of the world would appear to be such a problem. Indeed, in the earliest stages of the history of Philosophy in Greece, the problem of life seems to have been that which first presented itself as pressing for solution ;[1] and it still remains[2] one of the most central questions.

(c) We have seen that both Geology and Biology leave some of their ultimate problems to Chemistry. But Chemistry also is simply one of the special sciences. This fact is perhaps rather more apparent in the case of Chemistry than in the case of Biology. It deals only with a limited province, omitting, for instance, the question of

---

[1] The selection of water, air, etc., as fundamental principles by the early Greek philosophers was apparently due very largely to the fact that they were chiefly anxious to explain the origin of life.

[2] See, for instance, Ward's *Naturalism and Agnosticism*, Vol. I., pp. 177, 200, 291 ; Vol. II., pp. 27-29, etc.

life altogether; and even within that limited province it is not its business to clear up the ultimate meaning of the conceptions with which it works—such as those of force, mass, change, etc.—which it passes on to Physics. The problem of composition is no doubt peculiarly its own; but even this would seem in the end to be a physical problem.

(d) Most of the conceptions that have now been referred to, are no doubt more definitely dealt with by Physics; and it might be thought that here at least we reach what may fairly claim to be more than one among many special and limited sciences. Here, it may be said, we come at last to the consideration of ultimate conceptions, which are applied in all other natural sciences, and which it is the business of this science definitely to clear up. And certainly it seems to be true that the science of Physics is more closely related to Philosophy than most of the other special sciences are. Some of the early systems of Philosophy, such as that of Democritus, are little more than attempts to solve the fundamental problems of Physics, just as some still earlier systems were attempts to solve those of Biology;[1] and the name Natural Philosophy, which still clings to the science of Physics in some places,[2] may serve as an indication of the difficulty that has been experienced in separating off this branch of science from general philosophical speculation. It is more particularly that part of Physics which is known as Mechanics that is apt to claim to be something

---

[1] In early Greek Philosophy the general line of advance would seem to be from general Biology and Meteorology through Physics and Mathematics to Logic, Psychology and Ethics.

[2] Cf. p. 1, note 2.

more than a special science. The notion of a mechanical theory of the Universe[1] has often presented itself, even in quite recent times; and it does not seem, at least on a first view, to be in itself so absurd as would be a chemical or a biological theory of the Universe.[2] Yet a little reflection upon the subject-matter of Physics, as studied at the present time, makes it apparent that even this science is limited in its province, and does not press its conceptions to their ultimate issues. It may well be doubted, for instance, whether the existence of life or even of chemical properties could ever be completely explained by any mechanical theory, and it certainly seems clear that mental processes cannot be dealt with in this way. Again, it is not the business of Physics to bring out the ultimate meaning of such conceptions as those of number, space, etc.; and even force and motion need not be pressed by it beyond the region of working hypothesis, though the speculative physicist[3] will naturally try to have as complete an understanding of them as possible. What is true of Physics seems to be on the whole that, like Biology, it brings to light some ultimate problems for Metaphysics, but does not itself seek to solve them.

---

[1] See below, Book III., chap. ii.

[2] Nearly all the early philosophers of Greece, however, tended to think of the Universe in general on the analogy of a living being. Even with Plato, according to the view set forth in the *Timaeus*, the world as a whole is supposed to be formed in the image of the αὐτὸ ὃ ἔστι ζῷον.

[3] Such as Mach; see his book on the *Science of Mechanics*. On the general limitations of physical conceptions, reference may be made to Stallo's *Concepts of Modern Physics* and Ward's *Naturalism and Agnosticism*.

(*e*) The mathematical sciences, and especially Arithmetic, may be said to be even wider in their scope than Physics. For even purely mental processes may be numbered. But the limitation of the point of view in all such sciences is very apparent. No modern philosopher is likely to repeat the Pythagorean paradox, that the essence of things consists in mathematical determinations.[1] Moreover, even apart from their limitation of view, it does not appear to be the business of such sciences, any more than of Biology or Physics, to investigate the ultimate significance of the conceptions with which they deal—such as those of number and space.

(*f*) Psychology is another subject that has long claimed a place among the philosophical sciences, and that is still commonly included as one of the subjects of study in philosophical courses. And indeed it may be maintained of it, as of Arithmetic, that, in a certain sense, it includes everything within its province. "All the choir of heaven and furniture of the earth," everything that can become an object of experience at all, is capable of being regarded as one of the facts of consciousness,[2] and so of falling within the scope of psychological treatment. But here also, as in the case of Arithmetic, the point of view is a limited one, since these facts of experience are treated simply as appearances within some individual consciousness.[3] It may, indeed, be urged that this is a much more fundamental point of view than that of Arithmetic ; and the view that everything is simply a 'state of consciousness' can be more

---

[1] This was evidently the meaning of their saying that ' All is Number.' See Burnet's *Early Greek Philosophy*, pp. 307 *sqq.*

[2] See Berkeley's *Principles of Human Knowledge.* Part First, § 6.

[3] See Dr. Ward's article on Psychology in the *Encyclopaedia Britannica*, opening paragraphs.

plausibly maintained, and has in fact persisted longer than the view that "all is number." Yet no one is really content to remain at the point of view of Solipsism, to which such a doctrine appears inevitably to lead. In some sense and in some degree every one is constrained to admit [1] that we can speak of and can at least try to attain to the knowledge of a kind of reality which is more than a passing phase in the consciousness of some individual. Moreover, in this case once more, apart from the limitation of view, it appears to be the case that Psychology works with conceptions which it does not press to their ultimate issues. It may be urged, no doubt, that a complete Psychology must say all that can legitimately be said about such experiences as are described by the terms, Feeling, Sensation, etc.; since these cannot possibly be anything but what they are experienced to be, and it is the business of Psychology to find this out completely. But, even with reference to such experiences as these, our interest is not confined to their simple appearance in consciousness. We wish to understand their relations to other aspects of experience; and no Psychology does this completely, nor does it even appear to be the business of Psychology as such to attempt it. Psychology hands on such problems to Metaphysics, just as Arithmetic hands on the ultimate problems about number, Physics those about motion, and Biology those about life.

(g) But what shall we say about Ethics? In a sense it seems clear that the province of Ethics is limited. It deals

---

[1] Hume is practically the only one who has made a serious attempt to avoid this admission; and his view is frankly sceptical, i.e. it does not pretend to explain the possibility of a system of knowledge. Berkeley recognised the reality of minds, in addition to their conscious states.

only with one aspect of human life. The fixed stars at any rate are beyond its scope ; and even in the life of man on this planet, there is much with which it does not concern itself. From this point of view its claims to be regarded as philosophical seem to be distinctly less than those of Psychology or Mathematics, or perhaps even than those of Physics or Biology. On the other hand, it may be urged that some of the problems raised by Ethics are of an exceedingly fundamental kind, and are of a kind that it cannot pass on to any other science. It raises, it may be said, the question of the fundamental distinction between good and evil, right and wrong, and makes use of the conceptions of Duty, Obligation, Law, and others of a similar kind, which no other science seems to employ in quite the same sense. This, however, does not appear to be wholly true. The conceptions thus used by Ethics are largely similar to, and perhaps to a considerable extent identical with, those used by Logic, and possibly by all normative sciences. If there is anything strictly peculiar to Ethics, it would seem to be only the conception of absolute obligation ; and it appears to be possible to develop at any rate the greater part of the positive content of ethical science without any ultimate analysis of this conception. Hence, although it may be more difficult to avoid ultimate conceptions in Ethics than in most other sciences, yet it may be urged that in the end it is not only limited in scope, but refers the most fundamental problems involved in its subject-matter to some other science.[1]

---

[1] See below, Book III., chap. v. For discussions of the bearing of Metaphysics on Ethics I may refer to Mr. A. E. Taylor's article in the *International Journal of Ethics* (Vol. X., No. 3), and to his recent work on *The Problem of Conduct*.

(*h*) Similar remarks seem to be applicable even in the case of Logic, which is in many respects a science of the same type as Ethics. It has already been indicated that the problems presented by this science are to some extent identical with those contained in Ethics. It may be urged, however, that Logic is more directly responsible than Ethics for the final account of the conceptions that arise in its treatment, since it may be said to be the essential business of Logic to discuss the valid use of conceptions. But, at any rate, it is only a special kind of Logic that is concerned with this : Logic, as commonly understood, contents itself with the discussion of validity from particular points of view. Hence it is only in one of its special senses that Logic can be held to deal with ultimate ·problems, and in that special sense it appears to be practically indistinguishable from Metaphysics.[1] In any other sense it is simply one of the special sciences.

These illustrations may suffice to enable us to see what is meant by the general distinction between Metaphysics and the special sciences. The latter, in all cases, are limited in their scope, and evade the ultimate problems which their subject-matters suggest. Metaphysics, on the other hand, aims at completeness of view, and seeks to press all its questions home. Some further remarks, however, seem now to be called for on the exact relation between Metaphysics and such special sciences as have now been referred to.

---

[1] Logic, as understood by Hegel or by Dr. Bosanquet, can scarcely be distinguished from Metaphysics. Reference may be made on this point to the articles on Logic and Metaphysics in the *Encyclopaedia Britannica*, and to the recent book by Mr. J. B. Baillie on *The Origin and Significance of Hegel's Logic*, especially chap. **v.**

2. Relation of Metaphysics to the Special Sciences. It seems clear, at the outset, that Metaphysics cannot simply be treated as an Encyclopaedia of the sciences. The defect of the special sciences does not simply consist in their isolation or limitation. It consists much more in the fact that they are content with a point of view that is not fully analysed and understood. Hence, even if they could all be put together, so as to form a single comprehensive science, the incompleteness of the result would be rather emphasised than removed. Such a science might be called a whole, but it would not be an intelligible unity. Accordingly, the most important task for Metaphysics is that of sifting the ultimate conceptions that are left over by the special sciences, rather than that of directly attempting to bring the various special sciences together. Hence those sciences that make some attempt to deal with ultimate conceptions stand in a closer relationship to Metaphysics than those that pass on to others all the ultimate conceptions that are contained in them. Thus, such sciences as Physics, Biology, Mathematics, Psychology, Ethics, and Logic, may be called philosophical or metaphysical sciences ; and some of them may be said to be more so than others. If we finally define Metaphysics as the science which seeks to take a comprehensive view of experience, with the view of understanding it as a systematic whole, the general relation of such a science to other sciences ought now to be sufficiently apparent. But, in order to see more precisely what it involves, we must consider the exact sense in which the term experience is here used.

3. Meaning of Experience. The term experience, as here used, conveys practically the same meaning as the

phrase 'the Universe as such,' in the widest sense in which
that phrase can be used.   There are three main reasons,
however, for regarding the latter expression as less satisfactory than the term Experience.

One is that, when we speak of the Universe as a whole,
we are apt to be understood in a sense that does not
really include everything.   The feeling of pleasure or pain,
for instance, or anything else that is conceived to be purely
subjective—such as hopes, wishes, illusions, and the like—
would often not be regarded as falling within the content of
the real Universe.   The latter term is apt to be understood
as referring to that which is purely objective, in distinction
from the subjective experiences of any particular conscious
beings.   Yet these subjective experiences must equally be
regarded as part of that complete whole which the meta-
physician seeks to understand.

Further, when we use the term Universe, it is apt to be
understood as including much that lies or may lie beyond
all possibility of knowledge.   The real Universe may even
be conceived as consisting mainly of what Kant described
as 'things in themselves,' which are quite beyond the reach
of our faculties of apprehension.   Now, it is well to
recognise at the outset—what must surely be clear enough
in itself—that, if there is any such region of unknowable
things,[1] it cannot fall within the province of Metaphysics or
any other science to attempt to explore that region.   But it
is apt sometimes to be supposed (and this view has been
partly encouraged even by Kant) that this is just what the
science of Metaphysics seeks to do—to know the un-

---

[1] Of course I do not mean to deny here that the result of metaphysical
inquiry may be to lead us up to something unknowable or inscrutable.
As we shall see later, there is a sense in which this appears to be true.

knowable, to apprehend the inapprehensible. The use of
the term Experience may serve to guard from the first
against any such misconception.

Finally, the use of the term Experience suggests at once
the point of view from which it seems necessary to approach
our subject. If we simply set out with an attempt to
understand the Universe, we seem to be without a ποῦ στῶ ;
or rather we seem to be embarking on an infinite sea
without compass or rudder. The term Experience suggests
at once our point of departure—the consciousness of some
individual mind—and so provides us with something of
the nature of a guiding principle. It is here perhaps more
than in anything else, that modern philosophy has an
advantage over that of ancient Greece. Whatever may
be the differences among modern philosophers in other
respects, all are practically at one in this, that what we
have to seek to understand is the content and implications
of our conscious experience.[1] This we owe to Descartes,
more than to any other man ; but indeed it was the point
to which Greek Philosophy itself led up.

It might be urged no doubt, on the other side, that the
term Experience is also in danger of carrying with it certain
misleading associations—associations which are to a large
extent of the opposite kind to those suggested by the term
Universe. It tends, it may be said, to suggest to us what
is purely subjective, what simply belongs to some individual
mind, and so to set us off on a psychological method of
inquiry. This is true to some extent ; and it brings out a

---

[1] Dr. Shadworth Hodgson has written a *Metaphysic of Experience*,
which he contrasts with other recent systems. But Dr. Bradley's
Appearance and Reality, or the construction suggested in Dr. Caird's
Critical Philosophy of Kant, is also a Metaphysic of Experience.

danger that has been felt a good deal in the course of modern speculative thought. Perhaps the phrase " Universe of Experience " would, for this reason, be more satisfactory for our purpose than either of the two rival terms can be by itself. But, when we bear in mind that our inquiry is one that seeks to attain to completeness of view, and grasp reality as a whole —and even, in a sense, what is unreal or merely apparent—there cannot be much danger of supposing that we are simply to study the content of an individual consciousness as such ; so that even the use of the term Experience by itself is not likely to be very misleading.

4. **Forms of Experience.** When, however, we say that we are to begin from the point of view of conscious experience, the questions at once suggest themselves : *Whose* conscious Experience ? and *What aspect* of conscious experience ? The former question may perhaps be answered by saying at once that it must be the conscious experience of the person who is studying the subject. That must be the starting point, whatever he may ultimately reach. On the other hand, it must be remembered that the hope of arriving at any satisfactory results depends on the conviction, that this conscious experience is not in its essential features peculiar to the individual. Some recognition of the universality of consciousness is presupposed.[1]

As regards the other question, very little reflection on the world, as it presents itself to us in consciousness, is required to see that experience has very different levels, and very different degrees of significance for us. Thus, we find in our experience what have already been referred to as its more purely subjective aspects. The consciousness of pain

---

[1] See next chapter.

may be taken as one of the most striking types of these;
but any form of sensation [1] might suffice to illustrate it.
Such experience has been recognised even from very early
stages of philosophic development as dependent on individual peculiarities, and as having comparatively little
significance with reference to the Universe as a whole. [2]
Yet it cannot be overlooked in any complete attempt to
understand experience. On a somewhat higher level than
this must be reckoned our consciousness of particular
objects and events; yet even here we are in a region where
illusion and misconstruction readily enter in, and where
much depends on the peculiarities of the individual consciousness. In contrast with all this, we may refer to the
systematic experience of a man who is skilled in some
particular art or profession, or who has an extensive
knowledge of some particular branch of science. Everything that is contained in such a form of consciousness
has a certain universality of significance. Reflection on
such distinctions leads us to recognise three main levels
of conscious experience—sense experience, perceptual experience, and conceptual experience. Again, at all these
levels we are able to distinguish between the more purely
receptive sides, the more affective sides, and the more active
sides in our experience. Now, the analysis of these, and the
tracing of their relations to one another in the growth of the
individual conscious life, belongs properly to the province of

---

[1] Physical pain (aches and the like) seems to be, strictly speaking, a
sensation—not mere feeling.

[2] I am far from meaning to imply that such experiences are merely
subjective, or that they are wholly without significance from the point
of view of the universe as a whole.

psychology.[1] But a consideration of the general aspects of experience, as it presents itself in these various phases, may serve to bring out the nature of the problem that now lies before us. Accordingly, we proceed in the next chapter to the consideration of these general aspects.

---

[1] The student who has not pursued a course in Psychology ought to read some such work as Stout's *Manual of Psychology* before proceeding farther.

CHAPTER II.

GENERAL NATURE OF EXPERIENCE.

1. Aspects of Experience. Experience, as here understood, is a term of such wide significance that it may well seem hopeless to attempt to deal with it as a whole. Yet there are some fundamental aspects of it that we may at least profitably consider, with the view of throwing light upon its general nature. We may note, in the first place, what is of the utmost importance for our present purpose, that experience is at once universal and individual. The experience of all of us has a certain unity, of which we become more and more profoundly conscious through the extension of social intercourse. It is one world that we all know, and of which we all are parts. If doubt were thrown on this, not only metaphysics, but all other science, would become an impossibility—even the science of psychology.[1] Yet, on the other hand, the experience of each one of us is emphatically *mine*. There is something in it which we can never communicate to any other; and even what we do

---

[1] See the article on Psychology in the *Encyclopaedia Britannica*, p. 38. Psychology, as Dr. Ward says, must be " objective in the sense of being true for all."

communicate can be apprehended by another as it is for us only in so far as he learns to put himself in our place. This leads us to note that the experience of each of us, even when we consider it without special reference to any one else,[1] has a subjective and an objective aspect. We are aware of a world presented to us, which seems somehow independent of our individual apprehension ; and we are aware, at the same time, that it is presented to *us*. Further reflection leads us to note those fundamental aspects of our experience which are emphasised by psychologists—in particular, its apprehensive aspect, its feeling aspect, and its conative aspect. Psychology studies them simply as facts in our conscious life, appearing in different forms at different levels in the growth of our experience. It is for us here rather to try to understand the ultimate significance of these aspects of consciousness in relation to our experience as a whole.

Now, it seems clear that the most fundamental point in all this is the antithesis between self and not-self. It is this that stands out prominently, whether we have regard to the opposition[2] between the individual and the universal, between the subjective and the objective, or between our apprehension, feeling, and activity, and that which we

---

[1] Whether we could ever become aware of this antithesis, without reference to the consciousness of others, is a question that we need not here raise. Nor is it necessary at this point to discuss the question, whether the antithesis between the subjective and the objective means in the end anything else than that between the individual and the universal. *Prima facie*, it is a different point.

[2] The general fact of opposition is all that we are here concerned with. Whether these different ways of putting it imply different forms of opposition, is a question that we do not at present raise.

apprehend, feel about, and act upon. The most essential feature in all this is the fundamental duality of our conscious experience.

2. **Duality of Experience.** It may be doubted whether this element of duality is ever absent at any level of conscious experience. It may be that in mere sentience[1] there is no such distinction. There may be such a condition of consciousness as is described by the term coenaesthesis, in which there is mere qualitative awareness,[2] without its being an awareness of anything. But it is difficult to attach any intelligible meaning to such a condition. It is, at any rate, hardly to be found in our human experience. Here we seem always able to detect the antithesis, which we may express either by saying that there is a unity of focus, on the one hand, and a manifoldness of presented content on the other; or by saying that there is a manifoldness of conscious content on the one hand, and one world on the other hand, to which we refer it.[3] This antithesis appears no doubt most definitely at the higher levels of our conscious experience in which we have learned to reflect upon ourselves. It is only at this stage of development that we think of a systematic world of objects as existing with a certain relative permanence and independence, over against the processes of our own conscious life through which that world is apprehended and reflected upon, and which also

---

[1] For some discussion of mere sentience, from this point of view, reference may be made to Bradley's *Appearance and Reality*, p. 105.

[2] I.e. a consciousness containing distinctions that are not recognised by itself, but only by some other consciousness looking on and studying it.

[3] It is important to bear in mind that the unity, as opposed to the manifoldness, may be referred either to the subjective or to the objective side—either to the self or to the world.

has its own inner unity. But, even where this sharp contrast is not actually present, our own joys and sorrows, hopes and fears, fancies and illusions, and even systems of thought-construction, seem always readily distinguishable from those elements in our experience which we definitely ascribe to the world of objective fact, with regard to which we expect every one to agree with us. It is difficult to believe that such an antithesis is wholly absent, even in the animal consciousness. There is, at any rate, a strong *prima facie* presumption in favour of the view that this fundamental dualism is to be found in some degree at every stage of conscious experience.

3. **Subject and Object**. Reflection upon this duality of experience leads naturally to the idea of some form of interaction. Objects come to be thought of as making impressions on the conscious subject, or at any rate as somehow presented to it ; and the conscious subject is thought of as reacting upon them so as to produce changes in their states. The subject is thus itself converted into an object. It comes to be regarded as one thing among others,[1] standing in a relation of reciprocal action to the other things by which it is surrounded. The difficulties created by this way of thinking are evaded by the ordinary empirical sciences. Physical science seeks to confine itself entirely to the objective world, and raises no questions with regard to the subject to which objects are presented. Psychology, on the other hand, seeks to confine itself to the analysis of subjective processes, and avoids, as far as possible, any question

---

[1] I mean that this is a natural and almost inevitable transition in our thought. We are not at present concerned with the question, whether it may ultimately be possible to avoid such a transition.

as to the sense in which the subject exists, or as to the way in which it is related to the objects by which it appears to be affected, and upon which it appears to react. But it is the business of Metaphysics to face this ultimate problem. The question thus presents itself—Are there in reality two kinds of existence in the world of our experience? Is there, on the one hand, a world of objects, and, on the other hand, a world of subjects to which objects are presented? When the problem is stated in this way, however, we have, in fact, objectified both members in the antithesis;[1] we regard both as facts in the objective world; and the contrast is no longer that between subject and object, or self and world, but rather that between mind and matter.

4. **Mind and Matter**. When Mind and Matter come to be thought of as two different kinds of thing, the contrast between them is no longer quite the same as that between Subject and Object. The latter antithesis is a fact within our experience: the former is rather a theory to account for it. Yet the transition is very easy from the one point of view to the other. It is difficult to rest satisfied with the recognition of subject and object as two contrasted aspects of experience. The natural desire for something definite and solid to concentrate our attention upon, leads us almost inevitably to the substantiation of both members in the antithesis. They thus come to be thought of, not as two aspects of the unity of experience, but as two distinct things. Then we begin to note that they are, at any rate, two things of very different kinds. The general nature of the contrast

---

[1] This step is taken by Descartes, for instance, when he passes from his *cogito ergo sum* to the conception of a *res cogitans*, and from that to a *res extensa.*

between them is not difficult to point out. Mind presents
itself emphatically as a unity. It is the focus to which all
experience is brought. It is easy to distinguish aspects in
it, but hardly to distinguish parts. Matter, on the other hand,
is an aggregate. Even its qualities seem to a large extent to
depend on quantitative differences. It is essentially extensive, just as mind is intensive. Thus it is easy to pass from
the antithesis between subject and object in consciousness to
the contrast between two worlds, the world of mind (of which
consciousness then comes to be thought of as a quality),
and the world of matter (which then comes to be thought of
as independent of consciousness altogether). Thus we are
led directly to a dualism, such as that of the Cartesians.

5. **Unity of Experience.**   But, however natural this line
of thought may be, a little reflection is enough to show that
it is a very dubious one. For while it is true that all
experience seems to reveal a fundamental antithesis, it is
equally true that it never seems to reveal any separation.
On the subjective side we never, as Hume put it,[1] "stumble
on ourselves," in separation from a world of objects by
which the more purely subjective state is conditioned. On
the other hand, the objective side seems equally inseparable
from the subjective. We can know nothing of any material
world that is not somehow presented to consciousness, and
so is in some sense a fact of consciousness ; and the contention of Berkeley has at least a *prima facie* plausibility,
that there can never be any real justification for the doctrine
of the independent existence of material substance.[2]   The

---

[1] *Treatise of Human Nature*, Book I., Part IV., sect. vi.

[2] Even within the Cartesian school itself, the independent existence
of material substance practically disappears in the theory of Male-
branche, and never quite recovered itself again.

naïve dualism of ordinary experience readily gives place to an almost equally naïve idealism. It is here, then, that the real problem emerges—how to reconcile the apparent duality of experience with its equally apparent unity.

6. **The Problem of Metaphysics.** Such considerations may suffice to make the general nature of the metaphysical problem apparent. What it seeks to do is to consider the fundamental aspects of experience as a whole, and to try to understand the true relations of these aspects to one another. The questions which it raises are such as these— In what sense is our experience a unity, and in what sense is it a manifold? In what sense is it subjective, and in what sense is it objective? In what sense is it individual, and in what sense is it universal? The general meaning of these questions ought now to be clear. If we can make any approach to a satisfactory answer to them, or even to see clearly where the ultimate difficulties lie, there can be little doubt that we shall be able to throw a great deal of light upon the nature of our world and upon the significance of human life. This is what the science of Metaphysics aims at. It 'bakes no bread,' nor does it bring any new facts to our knowledge. Its problem rather is to make our world as a whole intelligible, to show us what all facts mean and what all bread is worth.

But, before we make any attempt to face this problem directly, it may be convenient to take a general survey of some of the most considerable attempts that have already been made in this direction. When we have seen the strong and the weak points of these, we may be in a better position to secure a standing ground for ourselves, or to see in what direction such a standing ground is to be sought.

CHAPTER III.

THEORIES OF METAPHYSICS.

1. **Dualism**. It can hardly be doubted that the dualistic theory is the one that commends itself most readily to ordinary common sense, at least in modern times. Among the ancient Greeks, no doubt, the earliest tendency of speculation was towards what must, in modern language, be characterised as Materialism ;[1] and, on the other hand, Oriental speculation perhaps tends most naturally to a vague Idealism. But the modern Physical sciences have discouraged the latter, and have not greatly encouraged the former. They have tended more and more to give us the impression of the possibility of a clear and complete view of the material world, in which all direct reference to consciousness is omitted. Such a view no doubt leads readily to the doctrine that consciousness is a mere "epiphenomenon," as the phrase is, in relation to the material system. But the view to which we are more naturally led is that of two diverse worlds each complete within itself. Accordingly, it is not

---

[1] In Professor Burnet's book on *Early Greek Philosophy* this tendency is probably exaggerated ; but his general contention seems to be a sound one. Early Greek speculation reached its most logical outcome in Atomism.

surprising that at the beginning of modern physical inquiry we find, on the philosophical side, the clear-cut Dualism of Descartes and his school, taking the foremost place among speculative systems. But the development of this school brings out in the clearest way the fundamental difficulties that are involved in such a conception of the universe. For the details of this development reference must be made to histories of Philosophy. It is enough for our present purpose to call attention to the one essential point which this line of development brings home to us, viz. : that, if we absolutely separate Mind and Matter, and regard them as two distinct worlds, it becomes impossible to understand the fact of their interaction, which yet is a fact that seems even more obvious to common sense than the fact of their distinction. Attempts to evade this difficulty by such theories as that of Occasionalism or of a Pre-established Harmony, lead us in the end to fairy tales of speculation,[1] which are more fascinating than convincing, and which are at any rate far removed from that contact with common sense which is the primary source of that strength of conviction which Dualism seems at first to carry with it. Such a system as that of Leibniz, indeed, can hardly be properly described as dualistic at all.

2. **Monism**. The Cartesian system, in fact, seemed to find in the end its direct logical outcome in the Monism of Spinoza. Monism, of the type represented by Spinoza, starts with the recognition of the *prima facie* reality of two distinct worlds, that of Mind and that of Matter, or that of Thought and that of Extension, but seeks to evade the problem raised by their relationship by affirming that, after

---

[1] Hegel applies this epithet to the philosophy of Leibniz.

all, they are one. This is so simple a way of removing the difficulty that, in one form or other, it has commended itself to many minds in recent times. The doctrine known as that of Psycho-physical Parallelism is the form in which it is now most familiar to us. In this form, however, it amounts to little more than treating the two aspects of the world as two, and then saying that they are one. What chiefly commends this view to men's minds is, that it enables them to treat Psychology, on the one hand, and the physical sciences, on the other, as independent subjects of study, while at the same time the ultimate problem of their relationship seems to present no difficulty. But these practical benefits can equally well be secured by saying that the problem of their relationship belongs to Metaphysics, without committing ourselves at the outset to any view as to the results at which Metaphysics may arrive.[1] Setting aside, then, the apparent practical convenience of the doctrine, we have to consider Monism on its own merits as a metaphysical theory. From this point of view, the difficulties that may be raised against it are very considerable. The fundamental antithesis between Mind and Matter cannot be got rid of by simply affirming that the two things are one. If they are one, why do they present themselves in two such diverse forms ? And if we say, not that they are one, but that they are parallel, what does this mean except (as has been suggested)[2] that they can never

---

[1] The discussions on this subject in the Psychologies of Höffding and Stout may be referred to. Though both these writers give their support to the doctrine of Psycho-physical Parallelism, their views of its ultimate significance are exceedingly different.

[2] Ward's *Naturalism and Agnosticism* (Vol. II., lecture xi.), where the whole subject of Psycho-physical Parallelism is very thoroughly discussed.

meet? In what other sense can that whose essential characteristic is its intensiveness be said to be parallel to that which is essentially extensive?[1] Spinoza's own system seems to fail utterly to show, either why there should be two aspects at all, or that there is any real correspondence between them. On the whole, it can hardly be regarded as anything more than an evasion of the difficulty presented by the apparent antithesis between the two worlds of Mind and Matter.

A much more satisfactory way out of the difficulty is that of denying the independent reality of one or other member of the antithesis. Indeed, this is what is sometimes meant by those who uphold the doctrine of Psycho-physical Parallelism. One of the two aspects is regarded as the mere shadow or epiphenomenon of the other. This view appears in the two forms of Materialism and Idealism, which we must next consider.

3. **Materialism.** As I have already indicated, a tendency towards Materialism is to be traced in some very early forms of speculation, notably among the ancient Greeks. But theirs is a naïve Materialism, comparable to that which appears in ordinary discourse when we speak of the force of a motive, the weight of a consideration, the breadth of a view. It arises rather from the difficulty of forming a definite conception of the non-material[2] than from any

---

[1] Merely to say that they undergo synchronous variations seems entirely unenlightening, unless we can point to some other correspondence than that in time.

[2] This is what perhaps Professor Burnet does not quite sufficiently recognise in the work previously referred to, e.g. in his treatment of the Eleatics. In a general way, however, he does very well bring it out. See especially p. 13. The Atomists seem to have been the first who

express attempt to explain the non-material in terms of the material. But perhaps all Materialism is, in this sense, more or less naïve. Any one who has once realised the fundamental antithesis between matter and thought can hardly hold the view that thought can be regarded as a mode of matter, *in the sense in which matter is contrasted with thought*. It cannot, that is to say, be regarded as a mode of motion or extension.[1] Materialism, in this sense of the word, is practically non-existent in modern times.[2] The view that thought is a mere epiphenomenon, as it is called, with respect to matter, is no doubt somewhat more respectable and much more prevalent. Yet it is difficult to attach any very serious meaning even to this doctrine. An epiphenomenon seems to mean something that appears over and above—a residuum ; and it is hard to see how Dualism is to be avoided by the use of such a phrase. At the most, it may lead us to regard consciousness as less primary and fundamental than matter ; but, from a meta-physical point of view, the degree of dignity that is to be ascribed to any element in experience does not seem to have much meaning. If consciousness is something other than matter, then, however secondary and trivial this something

---

definitely thought of the non-material as existent ; and they thought of it only as empty space. But, on the other hand, even the matter of the Atomists is thought of as capable of taking on curiously non-material modifications.

[1] I refer here to what are called the 'primary qualities' of matter. As regards the so-called 'secondary qualities'—colour, sound, heat, etc.—it would hardly be maintained by any one that these belong to matter, apart from its relations to mind.

[2] Writers like Tyndall, who say that Matter contains in itself "the promise and potency of all terrestrial life and thought," seem only to be giving utterance to the conviction of some vague ultimate Monism.

other may be, there yet remains a fundamental Dualism in our experience. The truth is, that to call consciousness an epiphenomenon, is only another way of saying that, in dealing with the purely physical aspects of experience, it is not necessary to take account of it; and this fact can be much more simply and directly expressed.

Materialism, in recent times, has tended to give place to Agnosticism. Instead of saying that the ultimate reality of things is to be found in Matter, in the sense in which Matter is opposed to Mind, the tendency is rather to say that the reality is to be found in something unknown (and perhaps unknowable) underlying both Matter and Mind. This view connects itself with Materialism, inasmuch as this fundamental reality is generally conceived as being more nearly akin to Matter than to Mind. This is, indeed, almost inevitable, from the very fact that it is thought of as unknown and unknowable, and so is at least foreign to consciousness.

4. **Agnosticism.** Agnosticism, like most of the other doctrines relating to ultimate reality, appears in several different forms. Its essential characteristic is the view that ultimate or self-subsistent reality[1] is not to be found in anything that actually appears in experience, but in something concealed behind experience, and inaccessible to thought. This differs from Scepticism in being a positive doctrine with respect to the nature of reality, not a mere attitude of doubt as to the possibility of knowledge. Traces of a doctrine of this kind may be found in early Greek

---

[1] The term 'reality' is very ambiguous. The reader must be warned to observe carefully the sense in which it is used at each point. I have done my best to make this clear.

speculation, where, however, it is in general hardly to be distinguished from Scepticism. It was Kant who first gave it an established place in thought as a definite theory of knowledge. According to him, we can only know the world as it is constructed for us through the determination of sense-data by the forms of consciousness. The world as thus known is only phenomenal, and the reality remains behind, beyond the reach of thought. A somewhat similar doctrine, though with a much less definite speculative basis, seems to have been maintained by Comte; and it appears to be one of the views that are put forward in the writings of Hamilton.[1] More recently it has been popularised in this country by Spencer and Huxley and their followers. The form in which it has gained most acceptance is that which is most simply summed up in the position, that we can know matter in terms of consciousness and consciousness in terms of matter, but that we can never know either as it is in itself, or the reality that underlies both. It is very difficult, however, to maintain the attitude of pure Agnosticism; and it may be doubted whether any one has succeeded in doing so. To know that we cannot know is almost an absurdity; for, in order to show the impossibility of knowledge, it is necessary to define that of which knowledge is sought, and it is hard to see how we can do this without knowing it. Accordingly, we nearly always find that those who maintain that ultimate reality is unknowable, yet hold that it can in some way or other be apprehended. The ' thing *per se* ' in Kant seems at first to

---

[1] Hamilton seems to waver between Natural Dualism and a certain form of Agnosticism. See Mill's *Examination of Sir William Hamilton's Philosophy*, p. 20 *sqq.* Also J. H. Stirling's *Sir William Hamilton.*

be something wholly removed from the grasp of thought;
but gradually, with the development of his system, it gives
place to the "Noumenon," which is at least an ideal of
thought; and in the end it appears to be capable in some
degree of apprehension by a kind of intellectual faith, though
not capable of being reached in the way of definite speculative insight; and even the Unknowable of Mr. Herbert
Spencer is regarded as sufficiently known to be characterised
as a Power, and indeed as something super-personal. Thus,
while the unknown reality appears at first chiefly as that
which underlies matter, it tends in the end to be thought of
rather as the ideal set up by consciousness; and, from this
point of view, Agnosticism may almost be regarded as a
bridge that carries us from Materialism to Idealism. It is
a kind of alembic whereby matter is first dissolved in mist,
to reappear as something that is more nearly akin to spirit.

5. **Idealism.** The simplest form of Idealism is that
which maintains that Matter has no independent reality,
but is simply a presentation to Mind.[1] This view seems at
first more revolting to common sense than that which
regards Mind as a mere mode of Matter; because Matter,
being the direct object of consciousness, seems at first to
have a more obvious substantiality than Mind. But a little
reflection suffices to remove this apparent substantiality of
Matter. It is easy to see that we can know nothing of
Matter except through the mental determinations to which
it gives rise; and if these determinations can be otherwise

---

[1] In the case of this, as of most other doctrines, it is difficult to point
to any one who maintained it in its naked form. Berkeley came near it
in his earlier writings, but gradually moved away from it. Hume also
moved away from it in the opposite direction—that of denying the
substantiality of mind.

accounted for, the independent existence of Matter is clearly a superfluous hypothesis, if it is even a hypothesis to which any definite meaning can be attached. Once this has been recognised, the theory of Berkeley seems a remarkably simple and attractive one. It is necessary, of course, to postulate a divine Mind, in addition to the human mind, in order to account for the apparently inflexible regularity of the world of nature; but this postulate does not seem to present any special difficulties; and, once it is granted, all the facts of the Universe fall beautifully into place.

But there are two points at which this theory proves unsatisfactory. Further reflection leads to the conviction that the divine Mind in this doctrine, as in that of the Cartesians, is a *deus ex machina* rather than a genuine solution of a difficulty. However true it may be that the existence of human minds and a divine Mind would suffice to account for all the universe that we know, yet at least within the divine Mind the world of nature must be thought of as existing as a more or less permanent system of determinations. Such a system of determinations may be in some sense a system of *thought*-determinations;[1] but, at any rate, it cannot simply consist of presentations to consciousness. The divine Mind may in some inexplicable way present[2] the world to

---

[1] Berkeley, in his later writings, brought this out very fully and clearly.

[2] It must be remembered that Berkeley's doctrine, at least in the form in which he first expounded it, involves the view of the material world as a system of ideas *presented to* or *set before* the conscious mind. Such a view of ideas, as distinct from the mind itself, is puzzling enough with reference to the individual consciousness; but it becomes doubly puzzling when the ideas come to be thought of as presented by one mind to another. Reid's criticisms were sound on this point.

us ; but the pre-existence of that world in the divine consciousness would seem to depend on modes of thought-determination that cannot be supposed to be simply presented.[1] Further, it seems clear that the same arguments that are valid against the independent existence of Matter without relation to consciousness are equally cogent against the independent existence of Mind without relation to a material system.   Hence the view to which we should ultimately be led is rather that of a system of thought-determinations than that of a collection of Minds and their presentations.   Such a view is sometimes described as Absolute or Objective Idealism, in contrast to the Subjective Idealism with which Berkeley at any rate begins.[2] But it may be less confusing to use the Kantian term Transcendentalism to describe it.

6. **Transcendentalism**.   Transcendentalism, as understood by Kant, is associated, as we have seen, with a kind of Agnosticism.   He held, broadly speaking, that, while the world, as we know it, is a system of thought-determinations, there is a reality behind it which is essentially unknowable, or at least knowable only by a kind of intellectual faith.

---

[1] In Berkeley's language, it depends on *Notions*, rather than on *Ideas*.   In more modern language, it is conceptual rather than perceptual.   Even Berkeley recognises that the concept or notion is not something presented to the individual mind.

[2] In the later developments of Berkeley's thought (in which the 'notional' side is emphasised) he seems to approximate to such an Absolute Idealism.   Berkeley is generally—but not quite fairly—interpreted in terms of his earlier statements.   The justification for it is that most of those who have been disciples of Berkeley—from Hume downwards—have followed rather his earlier than his later tendencies.   A philosopher is apt to be judged, not by the company he keeps, but by the company that keeps by him.

But subsequent thinkers, proceeding along the same general
lines of thought, have been led to the conclusion that there
is no real ground for the affirmation of any such unknowable
reality.   Transcendentalism then comes to mean that the
whole system of reality—and not merely the world as we
know it—is constituted by thought-determinations.   This
phrase, however—" constituted by thought-determinations "
—is a somewhat vague one, and is capable of very various
interpretations.   In some sense or other, it would seem to
be the view that has the best chance of proving ultimately
satisfactory ; but we have yet to ascertain what that sense is.
To interpret it satisfactorily, we must understand precisely
what is meant by a thought-determination ; and this throws
us back upon the consideration of the general nature of
thought, and in fact upon all those problems, the discussion of which is generally included under the term
Epistemology.

7. **The Critical Attitude**.   Our survey of the various
types of metaphysical theory has not led us as yet to any
positive conclusion, but it has perhaps served to indicate
where the strong and weak points of the various doctrines
lie ; and it ought at least to convince us of the importance
of hitting upon a satisfactory method of inquiry.   Transcendentalism, as understood by Kant, was particularly
strong in its emphasis on the need of an exact method of
investigation.   The method adopted by Kant was described
by him as critical, and has been called by others epistemological.   The significance of this we are now partly in a
position to appreciate.   Whether we accept the transcendental point of view, as represented by Kant or any of his
followers, or whether in the end we are led to reject any
such doctrine, it seems clear that all metaphysical specula-

tion must force us back upon the problem as to the meaning of our thought-construction of the world. To make the nature of this problem somewhat clearer, however, we must pass from the consideration of different theories of Metaphysics to the study of different methods of metaphysical investigation. In the meantime our attitude towards metaphysical theories must, at any rate in some sense of the word, be a *critical* one. We see that they all present serious difficulties, and force us back upon previous questions. The most satisfactory of them—the Transcendental—does not present us with any ready-made answer, but rather points to a line of inquiry and suggests a method. We are thus led to see that there must be a certain propaedeutic to any serious attempt at speculative construction. We feel, in short, the need of what Kant described as " Prolegomena to every future Metaphysic." We have to ask in what sense a science of Metaphysics is really possible, and by what method we may reasonably hope to arrive at a solution of its fundamental problems.[1]

---

[1] The importance of a methodical procedure in Metaphysics would seem to be the element of truth in the view of those who hold that Epistemology must precede Ontology. It does not appear to me, however, that the distinction is one that can be sharply drawn. What is wanted as a propaedeutic to Metaphysics is not a theory of *Knowledge*, but a theory of *Experience* ; and a *complete* theory of Experience would be a complete Metaphysics. All that seems possible is to distinguish the general consideration of Experience from special metaphysical constructions. See the discussions between Professors H. Jones and A. Seth in *Mind*, New Series, Vols. II. and III.

CHAPTER IV.

THE METHODS OF METAPHYSICS.

1. **Early Dialectic.** The earliest forms of speculation, even among the Greeks, are in general characterised by the absence of method. The first philosophers were "sages," who trusted to a kind of prophetic insight. Aristotle compared them to untrained boxers, who might occasionally make a good hit by accident, but had not really learned the rules of the game. Xenophanes may be taken as the type of these, he who "looked abroad upon the universe as a whole, and said that the One is God"; or again, Heraclitus, "the dark," he who said that "the thunderbolt steers the course of the Universe." Such oracular philosophies are to be found even now, and are not without their use. In speculation, as in action, a man often goes farthest when he does not know where he is going. But such adventures are very uncertain. One man may "go forth, like Saul, to find his father's asses, and find instead a kingdom"; but the opposite kind of experience is at least as likely. The early Greek philosophers, however, soon began to pay some attention to method. The Eleatic School was, perhaps, specially remarkable for the incentive which it gave to methodical study, and

especially for its introduction of the Dialectic Method,[1] which has since played so important a part in philosophical speculation. The whole subsequent course of Greek speculation, in particular, was very largely dominated by this method.

It is not certain whether Parmenides or Zeno was the first to make a definite use of Dialectic. It is certain at least that the subsequent growth of the method was largely influenced by the discussions of Socrates, and that it reached its culminating point in the school of Plato. The essence of the method, in its most developed form, lies in starting from a more or less inadequate presentation of some aspect of experience, bringing out its inadequacy by showing the contradictions that are involved in it, when understood as ultimately real and independent, and so suggesting a more adequate point of view, or at any rate emphasising the importance of searching for a more adequate point of view. This method rests on the ultimate presupposition that the real must be self-consistent; a presupposition that has been definitely brought out in what is perhaps the most thorough application of the method in recent times —Mr. Bradley's *Appearance and Reality.*[2] With Plato this method led up to the idea of the Good, or of the Final Cause; but, by his own confession, it was very difficult to form any clear conception of this, or of its relation to the particular facts of experience. The final tendency of the dialectic method was towards Scepticism,

---

[1] See Burnet's *Early Greek Philosophy*, p. 325.

[2] But even Parmenides may be said to have made this sufficiently explicit in his early statement of the principle of Identity. See Burnet's *Early Greek Philosophy*, pp. 184-5, 193-4.

in which ancient Greek philosophy ended ; and it can hardly be denied that, in the hands of its most notable recent representative, Mr. Bradley, it has something of the same tendency. Its negative side is generally more convincing than its positive. It is easier to show that any given point of view is more or less incoherent than that a thoroughly coherent one can be reached. In ancient times Scepticism was staved off for a time by the influence of Aristotle ; but with him the dialectic method was sub-ordinated to the genetic treatment of the concrete facts of experience. His philosophy was in general valuable rather for its definite establishment of the special philo-sophical sciences—Psychology, Logic, Ethics, Politics, etc. —than for the light which it threw on the ultimate problems of Metaphysics.

2. **The Dogmatic Method.** Modern Philosophy, unlike ancient, began with the attempt to formulate a method. This attempt was made, partly in opposition to the domin-ance of the Aristotelian system, and partly in the effort to find some safe-guard against Scepticism. The chief attempt of this kind was made by Descartes, who definitely set himself to the problem of finding some truth which it is impossible to doubt, and then using this as the basis for the construction of a philosophical system. In doing this, he was guided to a large extent by the method of Mathematics, and the influence of this method was no less conspicuous in the work of several of his followers—notably Spinoza and Leibniz. This school was characterised by Kant as *dogmatic*. It attempts to make progress in philosophical knowledge by the definition and analysis of conceptions.

The objections to such a method are pretty obvious. Even in Mathematics no real advance seems to be possible by mere definition and analysis;[1] but the simple character of the modes of relationship with which mathematics deals makes definition and analysis possible to an extent that cannot reasonably be expected in a subject that seeks to understand experience in its concrete completeness. It is vain to imagine, as the Cartesians did, that Self, Substance, Cause, the Infinite, are conceptions that can be dealt with in the same way as Point, Line, Circle, and the like. It is easy to state exactly what is meant by a point or a circle; the only difficulty is to grasp their intricate relationships to one another. It is just the reverse with philosophical conceptions. It is comparatively easy to understand their concrete relationships, as practically used in the constitution of our experience, but exceedingly difficult to grasp their exact meaning and ultimate significance. Hence the dogmatic or mathematical method in philosophy, in spite of the brilliant speculative constructions to which it gave rise, was soon completely discredited.

3. **The Psychological Method** The next important step in the development of philosophical method is one for which Locke is chiefly responsible. He took the *cogito* of Descartes more seriously than the latter had himself done. Descartes started from the " I think " as the one point of certainty, but at once proceeded to extract from this the ideas of Self, Substance, Cause, Perfection, and a host of others. Locke was more cautious. Starting from " I think," he simply sought to ascertain what is contained in the individual consciousness. He thus initiated the psy-

---

[1] This was very fully brought out by Kant. It is also more or less definitely recognised, from a very different point of view, by such writers as Hume and Mill. See, for instance, Mill's *System of Logic*, Book II., chap. vi., § 2.

chological method of inquiry. From the first, this method was characterised by caution and a considerable element of doubt; but it was only by degrees that its full significance was brought out. For Locke there was no real doubt as to the reality either of the self or of the material world, though much [1] as to the possibility of knowing anything about such high entities as the Infinite and Eternal, or even of the real meaning of finite substance. But Berkeley saw that if the one certainty is "I think," there can be no real reason for postulating the reality of anything but selves that think and the contents of their individual thought; and Hume saw that even the self might be eliminated as anything other than a focus of ideas. Nothing, then, can be affirmed but that ideas exist and somehow come to focus in consciousness. Thus the psychological method led, even more directly than the dialectical, to an absolute scepticism.

4. **The Critical Method.** It was in view of these results that Kant introduced his critical or epistemological method. By this method he sought to avoid the difficulties involved in direct ontological construction, on the one hand, and mere psychological analysis, on the other. He gave a new meaning, we may say, to the *cogito* of Descartes. He saw that the one great certainty with which philosophy has to start is the experience of a world, not the mere consciousness of his own mind by the individual thinker. Accordingly, he definitely raised the question—What does the experience of a world consist in, and what does it imply? He was thus led to devote attention to the manifold material given in sensation, to the forms of time and space, to the unity of

---

[1] Locke himself may have been satisfied with his efforts to remove these doubts. Certainly few of his successors have been satisfied with them.

self-consciousness, and to those modes of thought-determination which he called categories. But, in analysing these
aspects of experience, he was to a large extent guided by
the results, and even by the presuppositions of previous
thinkers; and, in particular, his account of the categories
was based on the analysis of the logical judgment given by
Aristotle, in spite of the fact that Kant's own view of the
nature and work of judgment was materially different from
that of Aristotle. In fact, the whole philosophy of Kant
broke down from the want of any satisfactory method of
discovering the categories.[1]

5. **The Later Dialectic.** Some of the followers of Kant
made strenuous attempts to supply his deficiencies. Hegel,
in particular, devised a systematic method, by which all the
categories or thought-determinations [2] could be evolved or
arranged. This method was to some extent a revival of
the old Greek method of Dialectic; but it was much more
systematic than the latter. Its main idea was that, by
starting with the simplest and most rudimentary conception
—that of mere Being—it was possible to advance, in a
regular order, to all the more complex conceptions, by the
simple expedient of bringing out the inner contradictions
involved in the simpler conceptions when taken by themselves. Hegel maintained further, that, when the categories
are thus systematically evolved, it becomes clear that they
are not simply determinations of the individual conscious-

---

[1] For a discussion of these points reference must be made to such
works as Caird's *Critical Philosophy of Kant*. See especially Book I.,
chap. iii.

[2] Hegel, in general, dropped the term category and used thought-
determination (*Denk-bestimmung*) instead. But many of his followers
have returned to the Kantian expression.

ness, or of the human consciousness in general, but are the necessary forms of all thought-determination, and are consequently the general determinations of reality—or at least of any reality that is capable of being experienced by a thinking being ; and if such a system of thought-determinations can be consistently worked out, there can be no real reason for supposing that there is any surd left over—any " thing in itself " that cannot be grasped by thought.[1]

How far such a systematic evolution of the categories is possible, we cannot here discuss. It is enough for our present purpose to urge that the method is not suitable for a preliminary investigation of the contents of experience, such as we are now engaged in. With the view of bringing this out, two remarks may be made. The first has been already suggested by the use of the alternative expressions above, " evolved " or "arranged." Sometimes the Hegelian method is represented as one by which the various thought-determinations can actually be evolved from the simple starting point in the conception of Being. At other times it is represented rather as a method by which the various thought-determinations may be systematically arranged, and by which their validity may be tested. On the former interpretation the importance of the method would be much greater than on the latter ; and no one who wished to find out the elements involved in our experience could afford to neglect it. But it seems to be generally recognised by the most competent exponents of the Hegelian method

---

[1] For a further account and discussion of Hegel's general position, reference may be made to Baillie's *Origin and Significance of Hegel's Logic* and M'Taggart's *Studies in the Hegelian Dialectic.*

that this is not the correct view.[1] If, however, the method is rather one for arranging and testing the fundamental conceptions that are used in our experience, it need not be the best method for the analysis of our experience or even for bringing out the general significance of the elements that are contained in it. The second remark that has to be made on Hegel's Dialectic is closely connected with this one. Once it is recognised that the Dialectic is not to be taken as a mechanical process by which all the categories can be evolved, the importance of the linear arrangement of them becomes doubtful. Even for the purpose of methodical arrangement, and for the testing of their validity, a freer mode of treatment may in many cases be preferable.

Further reflection on the use that has been made of the Hegelian method by its ablest exponents suggests another consideration. It is generally recognised that one of the directions in which the Hegelian method of treatment has been most successfully applied has been in the study of various forms of development—e.g. the development of philosophy, of political history, of morality and law, of art, of religion. Now, in the treatment of these various forms of development, an attempt has sometimes been made to apply the dialectic method in a somewhat mechanical fashion; but I believe it would be generally acknowledged that the most valuable results have not been reached in this way, and that often it has proved extremely mis-

---

[1] See M'Taggart's *Studies in the Hegelian Dialectic* (chap. i., especially pp. 16-24, also 48-50, 91-102, 135-147), and Professor Wallace's very interesting comments in *Mind*, Oct., 1896 (reprinted in *Lectures and Essays*, pp. 55 *sqq.*). Cf. also Baillie's *Origin and Significance of Hegel's Logic,* especially p. 357.

leading. This suggests the question, whether the value of the Hegelian method has not depended more on its being a genetic method than on its being a dialectic method. This question gets an added force when we remember that in ancient philosophy it was not the dialectic of Plato so much as the genetic treatment of Aristotle, that provided solid results. This consideration leads us to ask more definitely what is to be understood by a genetic method.

6. **The Genetic Method**. In the specialised departments of philosophic study it is comparatively easy to see the value of a genetic treatment; and, as we have already indicated, this was made abundantly apparent by Aristotle. The modern doctrine of evolution has brought this method into still greater prominence. But it is apt to appear that Metaphysics is just the department of study in which such a method is necessarily inapplicable. Here, it may be said, we deal with what is eternal, not with what is in process. Yet the Hegelian system, at least, has suggested the possibility of a genetic treatment even here. The whole of Hegel's Dialectic has a genetical character; and, as one of the most acute of his commentators has urged,[1] the process comes to be more purely one by development, and less one by dialectical opposition, as it advances. But further reflection on the nature of the problem that lies before us may make it still more evident that for us at least this method is almost inevitable.

What we seek to study is the general nature of our experience of the world. Now this, at least, is clearly a growth, and we can hardly hope to understand it except by observing its forms of development. It may be objected,

---

[1] See M'Taggart's *Studies in the Hegelian Dialectic*, pp. 121-134.

no doubt, that to do this is to adopt the psychological method, which has already been tried and found wanting. But this is not really the case. Such a method as is now suggested would, indeed, follow largely along the line of psychological study, but with a wholly different aim and point of view. The point of view is epistemological, and the aim is that of discovering what is ultimately real. In psychology, on the other hand, we try to study experience simply as a process going on in an individual consciousness. We try to set aside all questions with respect to validity or reality. We try to treat all experience as purely subjective. It was just for this reason that the old psychological method, as conceived by Locke and his followers, broke down. Their problem, we may say, was, Assuming that experience is essentially subjective, how does the element of objectivity enter in? And the answer, from the very way in which the problem is put, could hardly be anything else than that the element of objectivity is an illusion, an illegitimate addition to the materials with which we start.[1] For us, however, the problem does not present itself in this way. We ask— Given an objective experience, what account can we render of the significance of the various elements in its growth? We are to study the process of experience, not as process, not from the point of view of its origin and course, but rather from the point of view of what it becomes, from the

---

[1] This is the result as worked out by Hume. Whether the line of thought started by Locke might have been worked out to a different issue is perhaps one of those futile questions of 'what might have been' in history. There are no doubt in Locke's own writings indications of other directions in which his line of thought might have been developed. There are anticipations of Kant; and in his chief follower, Berkeley, there are even anticipations of Hegel.

point of view of what it has in it to be. We are trying to discover, in the significant Aristotelian phrase, its τὸ τί ἦν εἶναι, what it essentially was.

Is it really possible to study the process of experience in this way? This is a question that can only be satisfactorily answered by making the attempt.

7. **Plan of the Present Work.** This, then, is the task that we now definitely undertake. Without committing ourselves absolutely to the view that the method now suggested is the best method of study, we accept it provisionally as a statement of what is to be here attempted. Two grounds at least may be given for its adoption. It seems to be the method which was led up to by the development both of ancient and of modern philosophy: it keeps us in touch both with Aristotle and with Hegel. But further, what is still more important, it keeps us in touch with what was the main source of strength both in Aristotle and in Hegel—the concrete content of experience. If we fail to understand this content, we shall at least not be leaving it behind us.

What we have to ask, then, is—How does the experience of a world grow up, and what is the significance of the various elements in its development?

BOOK II. THE GENESIS OF EXPERIENCE.

CHAPTER I.

THE GENERAL NATURE OF CONSCIOUS GROWTH.

1. **The Problem re-stated.** The nature of our problem ought now to be sufficiently apparent. We are to try to understand the general significance of our experience as a whole by observing the process of its development. Yet it may well seem that a certain amount of obscurity still remains in the problem as thus stated. How are we to proceed, it may be asked, in investigating the significance of the various elements in our experience? What principles are to guide us in our analysis, and how are we to test the value of our results? Again, it may be said, if our study is really to be genetic, if we are actually to study our experience in the process of its growth, how can it essentially differ in the end from the similar study that is undertaken by the psychologist?

To the last of these questions the answer is, I think, simple enough, and has already been sufficiently given. It is our aim to study experience, not simply as a process in the individual consciousness, but in its general significance. This question is really as distinct from that of the psychologist as the question, "What is the general nature of Life?" is distinct from the question, "What are the leading types of plants and animals?" But, just as, in this instance, it would probably not be possible to make any real study of the nature of life without reference to the way in which life grows up in its particular forms, so it seems probable that one cannot really hope to understand the nature of experience in any other way than by the study of its development. But it must be our endeavour to do this in such a way as to subordinate the study of the special forms and accidents of conscious process to the attempt to grasp its essential characteristics. It will, I think, be found as we go on that the presence of this aim is quite sufficient to differentiate our study from that of the psychologist, though its close relation to the latter is not to be denied.[1]

If we accept this answer, however, it only seems to bring the previous inquiries into greater prominence. For it makes it more apparent that a merely genetic account, a simple attempt to trace the origin and growth of conscious experience, will not meet our requirements. But, if so, it may be asked, how are we to proceed? How are we to know what is significant and what is insignificant, what is essential and what is accidental, unless we have at the outset some criterion in our minds, some standard of value,

---

[1] On this point some papers by Professor Dewey in *Mind* (Old Series, Vol. XI., pp. 1 and 153) will be found very instructive. I differ somewhat from Professor Dewey, if I understand him rightly, inasmuch as I recognise that there is a place for Psychology as an empirical study, as well as for that kind of Psychology (if it is properly to be so called) which may be described as 'philosophic method.' The essential point, I think, is that the genetic method can with advantage be applied both to Psychology and to Metaphysics. The notable success of Aristotle in ancient times, and of Hegel in modern times, seems to me to be due very largely to their adoption of this method.

some test of reality? Ought we not, then, to begin with the inquiry into this?

The answer to this seems to be that, from the nature of the case, there can be no test or standard external to that which is here to be judged. It is through experience that we learn to distinguish the real from the unreal, the essential from the accidental; and it is only through the study of experience that we can understand what such distinctions mean. No test can be applied to experience as a whole but that of its own internal coherence. It is here that Hegel's famous reference [1] to Scholasticus is in place—the man who would not venture near the water till he had learned to swim. There is no province other than experience in which we can exercise our thought and provide it with standards of judgment. We must test our experience by itself. [2] Hence the only reply that we can make to such difficulties as have been suggested is a *solvitur ambulando*. We must venture into the water—gradually, no doubt, and cautiously —and see what progress we can make in it. We must take up experience as a concrete fact before us, and see how far it is possible to give a coherent account of it. In doing this we must, as in similar enterprises, make use of the attempts that have already been made by others, guiding ourselves both by their successes and by their failures, but not expecting any rules that will save us from the necessity of thinking out the problem for ourselves. If we succeed in our efforts, the evidence of our success will be found in the completeness of our insight into the nature of experience. If we fail, the

---

[1] *Encyclopaedia*, *Logic*, Introduction, § 10.

[2] The explanation already given of experience must be borne in mind. It means the universe as apprehended by us, not the mere subjective fact of apprehending it.

evidence of our failure will be no less apparent in the fact that we are left groping in the dark. No other standard or criterion is possible.

Let us begin, then, by looking once more at the general nature of the experience with which we have to deal.

2. **Experience as a Many in One**. As we have already noted, it seems to be one of the most fundamental characteristics of experience that a manifold content is focussed at a single centre. There is thus involved in it both a Many and a One. The oneness of it is frequently expressed by saying that it is one self or subject that knows ; the manifoldness, by saying that there are many objects presented to this single self. But this is a mode of expression that contains highly complex conceptions, and it is one that seems appropriate only to the more fully developed stages of conscious experience ; and even with reference to these it is somewhat misleading. From the point of view of the fully developed consciousness, the unity of experience is as much objective as subjective. It is one world that we know, quite as truly as it is one self that knows it. On the other hand, in less developed modes of consciousness, the opposition between the One and the Many would seem to be latent. In simple sentiency, such as we sometimes approximate to, and such as we may well suppose some other conscious beings approximate to still more closely, it may be doubted whether there is any such definite antithesis. Hence some have thought of the earliest and simplest form of experience as an undifferentiated unity. But it is hard to see how an undifferentiated unity could be a form of consciousness at all. There must, it would seem, be more or less of a

manifold in all actual experience.[1] Yet it would seem
equally impossible that any conscious experience should
merely consist of a manifold without any form of unifica-
tion.   A mere unity could not contain the consciousness of
anything; and a mere blank awareness seems meaningless.
A mere manifold, on the other hand, could not attain the
consciousness of anything ; and mere floating ideas, without
any point of reference, seem equally meaningless.   Hence,
though we may allow that the definite antithesis of subject
and object is a late growth, yet we seem bound to suppose
that in all forms and levels of conscious life there is something of the nature of a manifold in unity.   And it is on
this fundamental contrast in all conscious life that the
most essential aspects of experience seem to depend.

3. **Aspects of Conscious Life**.   Most psychologists
recognise, in some form or other, three main aspects of
conscious experience.   These are sometimes referred to
briefly as Knowing, Feeling, and Willing ; but it would
be generally acknowledged that this is a somewhat loose
way of marking the distinction, and a way that is, at the
best, appropriate only to the more highly developed levels
of conscious experience.   The essential points seem capable
of expression in the following way.

We have, first of all, the simple emergence of a manifold
content in consciousness.   This content is always somehow presented within a unity ; but there need not be any
conscious reference to such unity.   The presence of this
unity, however, shows itself at least in this way, that the
content presented is not bare and cold, but has always an
affective side.   It is felt as in harmony or in dissonance

See Bradley's *Appearance and Reality*, p. 106.

with the form of unity [1] within which it emerges; and this before there has been any conscious reflection upon that unity itself. Further, this consciousness of harmony or dissonance is seen, on reflection, to be connected with changes that take place from within in the content of our conscious experience. Thus we have the three elements, simple presentation in consciousness, feeling, and conscious activity (i.e. the reaction of the unity of consciousness on particular portions of its content). The exact meaning of these various aspects we cannot at present discuss. But it seems clear that at all levels of conscious experience they can, in some way or other, be distinguished. There is always some content in consciousness; that content always affects, agreeably or disagreeably, the consciousness in which it is; and there is always something of the nature of a reaction.

The significance of this may be made more apparent by a brief consideration of the various stages in the development of experience.

4. **Stages of Conscious Development.** There seem to be three clearly marked stages in the growth of experience —stages which are most simply marked by the terms Sensation, Perception, and Conception. We shall have to give some detailed attention to each of these, as we proceed. In the meantime, it is sufficient to notice their most fundamental characteristics.

---

[1] The unity here referred to, it must always be borne in mind, may be of very various kinds. It may simply be the functional unity of a particular sense organ; it may be the general unity of the organism, as reflected in consciousness; or, again, it may be a form of conative unity, constituted by a more or less definite plan or purpose; or it may be the unity of a conceptual scheme, some thought of life as a whole, or of a world or universe.

It is doubtful whether there is any such experience as one of pure sensation, but it is at least possible to approximate to this state; and there may be some forms of animal life in the consciousness of which hardly anything more is present. Such a condition would be one in which some simple content, such as a blue colour or a sweet taste, emerges in consciousness, without being referred to any object or in any way manipulated or interpreted by thought. In such a state as this, the antithesis between subject and object may at most be described as implicit; but the three aspects of consciousness, which appear to depend on this antithesis, are already present in a rudimentary form. The presentation of a simple sensation seems always to be accompanied by an element of agreeableness or disagreeableness, and there seems to be nearly always something of the nature of simple reaction in connection with it. The possibility of this appears to imply some rudimentary unity of consciousness (which of course need not be what afterwards comes to be known as the unity of the subject).[1] But everything at this stage tends to be implicit and undeveloped.

Perception, on the other hand, involves the bringing together of various facts of sensation, and the combination of them in definite objects.[2] This, of itself, implies a certain reaction of consciousness upon the simple material at first presented. The formed object may, however, be regarded as the datum, and elements of feeling and activity

---

[1] It may, equally well, be a vague anticipation of what afterwards comes to be known as the unity of the object.

[2] Which, however, are not to be thought of as constituted simply by the combination of sense-elements. An object is no more a mere combination of sensations than an animal is a mere combination of limbs.

may be noted as its accompaniments. The feelings that accompany the presentation of objects are much more complex than those that go with pure sensation. In such an animal emotion, for instance, as anger, the element of dissonance seems much more definite and highly developed than in simple pain.[1] Action also is, at this level, much more highly developed, and begins to be more of the nature of adjustment to ends, though the actual idea of an end may not be present. A being that has such a presentation of definite objects seems, moreover, to begin to be vaguely aware of the antithesis between itself and the objects that are distinguished from itself. But all this becomes much more explicit at the third stage.

At the level of Conception, there is not only the presentation of objects but the apprehension of these objects as related to one another in various ways. The content of consciousness becomes a system of relations, and, in connection with this, more developed forms of feeling and activity grow up. What are called the sentiments, for instance, are connected with such systems ; and action in which there is a definite thought of an end—voluntary action, in the full sense of the word—becomes for the first time possible at this level. Along with this comes the explicit recognition of the unity of the self, as against the world that is distinguished from it. Of course all this is gradual, and implies many subordinate stages of development.[2]

---

[1] So much so that some writers have even been led to deny that anger is in itself disagreeably toned. Cf. Stout's *Manual of Psychology*, p. 310.

[2] Pure Imagination, in particular, would seem to come between Perception and Conception ; but it is doubtful whether it can be recognised as a distinct stage. It would seem rather to be transitional in its nature.

These seem to be the main points in the three stages of conscious development. Some further details with regard to them will have to be considered later.

5. **Metaphysical Interpretation of Conscious Process.** Now it is the business of Psychology to analyse these various stages of conscious development, and to show how one leads on to another. Thus the passage from Sensation to Perception might involve the consideration of what have been called 'psychical dispositions'; and, in passing from Perception to Conception, it might be necessary to consider the part played by Imagination, in the widest sense of that term—i.e. the part played by imagery. But the detailed study of such processes is not the business of Metaphysics. Here we have simply to ask what elements these various modes of conscious development contribute to the apprehension of reality. Now, from this point of view, it is no doubt the latest and most developed stage that chiefly concerns us; for it is only at that stage that we learn to attach any definite meaning[1] to the distinction between the real and the merely apparent. But the consideration of the earlier stages seems essential for the right analysis of the later. For if the later contains the earlier within itself as an element in its more complete system, it seems equally true to say that there is nothing in the later that is not anticipated in the earlier, and that we shall get to understand it best by tracing out the way in which what is at first implicit becomes gradually unfolded. We may say, on the one hand, *Nihil in intellectu quod non prius*

---

[1] Of course even an animal must have a *practical* consciousness of the difference between the real and the illusory. It has its disappointments, its failures, its disillusionments.

in sensu, even if we have afterwards to add, *Nihil in sensu quod non melius in intellectu.* While, then, it is chiefly in thought-experience that we must hope for metaphysical enlightenment, yet the earlier stages cannot be neglected without serious danger of misconception and one-sidedness of view. Accordingly, we shall now proceed with the consideration of the three stages in order, endeavouring to note the nature of the apprehension of reality that is contained in each.

CHAPTER II.

SENSATION.

1. **Nature of Sense-experience**. Sense-experience is a fact so simple that it seems impossible to analyse it into anything more elementary, or to trace it back to anything more primitive than itself. Just for this reason its metaphysical importance is exceedingly great. Here at least, it may fairly be thought, we come upon the solid rock, upon what is most ultimate and rudimentary in experience. Even here, however, there are degrees in the character of the experience with which we have to deal. Some modes of sense-experience come before us with a more rudimentary appearance than others. What is called general sensation, for instance, seems more rudimentary than such highly specialised modes of sensation as colours and sounds. Some of the latter again appear to be more simple than others. White, for instance, seems more simple than purple.[1] The simplest of all modes of sensation is probably to be found in what is called coenaesthesis, the general

---

[1] Points of this kind have to be stated with great caution. There is constant danger of confounding complexity of stimulus, i.e. complexity in the physical or physiological accompaniments, with complexity in the sense-experience itself.

organic consciousness ; and yet, from another point of view, it is possible that this contains a combination of the elements that are separated out in the more special forms of sense-experience. It may be doubted, indeed, whether it is possible to point to any quite simple experience of sensation. The most rudimentary beginning to which we can go back seems rather to contain in it already the elements of that future complexity which emerges as experience grows. Some consideration of the leading characteristics that belong to sensations may help us, however, to an understanding of its general nature.

2. **Pure Sensation, and its Characteristics.** The following are the points that seem most noteworthy with regard to sensation :

(*a*) **Its Simplicity.** It may be doubted, as I have said, whether there is any such thing as an absolutely simple sensation ; but, at any rate, it seems clear that in pure sensation we approach more nearly to the simple than in any other aspect of experience. The only other aspect that could be compared to it in this respect is pure feeling ; but feeling always seems to relate itself to something other than itself. It is always more or less adjectival ; whereas sensation is of the nature of a substantive experience. When we experience pleasure, something is pleasant ; whereas the pure sensation of colour does not seem to contain in itself any reference to anything else.[1] Sensation, then, would seem to be, at any rate, the relatively simplest element in experience.

(*b*) **Its Passivity.** Sensation presents itself also as more

---

[1] Here again the statement has to be made with some caution. Of course in *perception* colour is referred to a coloured object.

purely *given* than any other aspect of our experience. We do not seem in any way to make it for ourselves. Here again pure feeling might be compared with it. But feeling is at least always on the way to action. What is pleasant tends to be chosen ; what is painful tends to be avoided ; and, even if feeling does not thus lead to an active readjustment, it seems at least to be always our way of relating ourselves to what is presented. We do not simply get something, but we also put ourselves in a certain attitude towards it. Thus, feeling can hardly be said to be passive in the same sense in which sensation is so. What exactly is meant by activity and passivity, we cannot now consider. But at least sensation seems to present itself as the relatively passive.

(*c*) **Its Distinctions**. In spite of the relative simplicity of sensation, there are characteristics by which different sensations can be distinguished from one another. It seems possible to distinguish sensations from one another in respect of Kind, Quality, and Degree. The significance of these distinctions must be somewhat more fully considered, but their general nature seems sufficiently apparent. Sound appears clearly to be a different kind of sensation from colour. Red is a different quality of colour from blue. A bright red is different in degree from a dim red.[1] Distinctions of this sort seem to be discoverable even in the simplest sense presentations.

(*d*) **Its Accompaniments**. All sensation, however simple it may be, appears to be accompanied by feeling. It

---

[1] Much care is required in characterising these distinctions. Brightness, for instance, as opposed to darkness, seems to be qualitative ; but, as opposed to dimness, it is a matter of degree.

is always, in some degree, experienced as being agreeable or disagreeable, and there seems always to be some degree of reaction along with this.

These elements are taken up directly from the results of psychological analysis. We must inquire a little more definitely what some of them mean. As regards simplicity and passivity, it does not at present seem necessary to add anything further; but the other points call for a little further explanation.

3. **Distinctions of Kind.** Distinctions of kind are the most fundamental. How many distinct kinds of sensation there are in our experience, is a question to which no precise answer can as yet be given. But colour, sound, taste, smell, pressure, temperature, perhaps organic pain, and possibly some others,[1] seem to differ from one another in kind—that is to say, the difference between them is abrupt, not one of gradual transition along a definite line. Hence it seems impossible in such cases to give any direct account of the nature of the distinction. We can only enumerate the various sensations, and state the conditions—physical and other—under which they arise.

4. **Distinctions of Quality.** Distinctions of quality differ from distinctions of kind in being not abrupt, but such that it is possible to pass from one to another by a continuous transition. We can pass from green to scarlet by imperceptible shades of difference, but no similar transition will ever carry us from scarlet to the sound of a trumpet. In the case of quality it is, accordingly, possible for us to give an account of one sensation in terms of another. We can say that orange is between red and yellow, and so on. Yet

---

[1] See Titchener's *Outline of Psychology*, pp. 59-65.

such accounts can only be given in terms of certain ultimate distinctions which, if taken separately, would seem to be distinctions of kind. If there were no intermediate shades, white and black, blue and red, sweet and bitter, would appear to be different kinds of sensation. The difference between kind and quality seems to depend on the possibility of a continuous transition.[1]

5. **Distinctions of Degree.** Degree is also continuous, but differs from quality in involving a transition not from one kind to another, but from zero to a certain amount. All sensation seems to involve degree, as Kant urged.[2] Whatever we experience is not zero and is not infinite, but has some finite intensive magnitude. It is doubtful, however, whether there is only one kind of degree in sensation, or several. Simple degree of sensation is generally called intensity ; but some have thought that there are other kinds of degree that may be called extensity and protensity, forming the basis for what, in the more developed consciousness, comes to be known as the apprehension of space and time.

6. **Feeling-tone of Sensations.** The pleasure and pain that accompany sensations are themselves closely akin to sensations. It is very difficult, for instance, to draw a sharp distinction between the feeling of disagreeableness and the

---

[1] In some cases, such as heat and cold, it seems doubtful to which class the distinction properly belongs. For in this case the transition from the one to the other is not made through a series of positive intermediate stages, but through a zero-point. The same is probably true of sweet and bitter. Yet there seems to be a certain continuity of direction in such transitions. They belong to a single system, in spite of the interposition of a zero-point.

[2] *Critique of Pure Reason*, Transcendental Analytic, Principles of Pure Understanding, II.

organic sensation of pain, or again between the feeling of agreeableness and the sensation of sweetness. Moreover, the pleasure-pain experience seems to resemble sensation in having distinctions of quality (the pleasant and the painful) and of degree (more or less intensity and possibly also protensity).[1] But it seems to differ from sensation by reason of its more secondary character. It is other sense-experiences that give rise to the feeling of agreeableness or disagreeableness, and this seems to involve a kind of primitive valuing of these sensations, or at least a reference of them to the unity of consciousness as in harmony or discord with it. Some say that pleasure-pain is not of the nature of presentation or conscious content at all; but this can hardly be true if it has quality and degree.[2]

7. **The Active Element in Sensation**. Feeling, as we have already noted, seems in itself to imply a certain re-action of the unity of consciousness upon its particular content. Such action at least seems to belong even to the lowest phases of conscious development, and may be opposed to the pure passivity or immediacy that appears to be characteristic of simple sensation. We are not yet in a position to consider further the nature of this fundamental antithesis between activity and passivity.[3]

8. **Metaphysical Significance of Sensation**. The chief point that has metaphysical interest with reference to sensa-

---

[1] It is particularly instructive to compare feeling with such sensations as sweet and bitter, hot and cold. These contraries (unlike black and white, red and blue) are connected through a zero-point. This seems to be the case also with the agreeable and disagreeable. Cf. Külpe's *Outlines of Psychology*, pp. 238-243.

[2] See below, Book III., chapter iv., § 2.

[3] See below, Book III., chapter iii., § 3.

tion is the question whether it contributes any ultimate element to experience, of which no further account can be given. According to the view of Kant, the manifold of sense is an ultimate datum with which thought has to deal, but of which thought can give no account. We are not yet prepared to consider how far this view is to be accepted. But it must be noted as one of the chief points presented by sense-experience for metaphysical consideration. Again, there is the question as to the ultimate meaning of distinctions of kind, quality, and degree. With regard to the first of these, J. S. Mill has pointed to distinctions of kind among sensations as containing the ultimate limits of possible explanation.[1] But it may be asked whether distinctions of quality do not contain something equally ultimate. Is there any more hope of understanding the distinction between sweet and bitter, or red and blue, than there is of understanding the distinction between sound and colour? Degree, again, is emphasised by Kant as the one element that can be foreseen *a priori* as necessarily belonging to all sensation. Space and Time seem to be implicitly contained in the extensity and protensity of sensations. Then there is the problem as to whether Feeling and Activity are ultimate and unanalysable elements in experience.

Now, we are not as yet in a position to discuss any of the metaphysical problems that are thus raised. But it is important that we should have them before us, so that we may not overlook any of them as we proceed. It may be well, therefore, to enumerate the points once more in order :

(1) The meaning of the " Given."

(2) The antithesis of the One and the Many.

---

[1] *System of Logic*, Book III., chapter xiv., § 2.

(3) The antithesis of Active and Passive.

(4) The meaning of Kind.

(5) The meaning of Quality.

(6) The meaning of Degree.

(7) The nature of Space.

(8) The nature of Time.

(9) The nature of Feeling.

All these problems seem to be involved, explicitly or implicitly, in simple sense-experience; but we shall be better able to appreciate their significance when we have noted the elements that come out in the further stages of conscious development.[1]

---

[1] The question whether there is actually a sensational level of experience, as distinguished from the perceptual, need not here detain us. The moth that flies into the candle can hardly be supposed to have much in the way of perception of objects; but whether any conscious being can be wholly without perception, is a more difficult question. We may at least say that there is an indefinite approximation downwards towards a purely sensational experience as a limit. Perhaps it is only an ideal limit, like Aristotle's πρώτη ὕλη. It may be noted that the complete realisation of a world for thought has a similarly ideal character. The perceptual consciousness is perhaps the stage of development that is most completely actualised. But even this would appear to be actualised in a variety of phases, rather than in one definite form.

CHAPTER III.

PERCEPTION.

1. Nature of Perceptual Experience. The perceptual level of consciousness lies midway between the sensational level and the thought level, and, being thus in the middle, has perhaps less direct metaphysical interest than either of the other two. It does not raise ultimate problems to the same extent as they do, since the material which it presents is neither at the beginning nor at the end of things. Yet it is at least worth while, for our present purpose, to consider its general characteristics.

As compared with sense-experience, it is at once apparent that it is lacking in simplicity. Nothing that we perceive can be taken as an ultimate datum : it can always be analysed into elements more primitive than itself.[1] Again, since it involves a synthesis of these more primitive elements, it is also lacking in that passivity that characterises pure sensation.

---

[1] I do not think this is necessarily inconsistent even with such a view as that put forward by Mr. Hobhouse in his *Theory of Knowledge* (Part I., chap. i.), according to which the primitive fact of consciousness is a mode of assertion. For we can at least ideally distinguish between the act of assertion (which is common to many contents) and the par-

On considering further the elements that go to make up our perception of objects, the following seem to be the points that call for special attention :

(1) The synthesis of the sense material.

(2) The presentation of a thing.

(3) The recognition of individual identity.

(4) The apprehension of change.

(5) The consciousness of space.

(6) The consciousness of time.

(7) The pursuit of ends.

All of these points come out more definitely at the thought level ; but the significance of the latter is perhaps made clearer by considering the process of development towards it.

2. **The Synthesis of Sense-material.** The synthesis of sense-material, by which the perception of objects is characterised, introduces in a more definite form the relation of the one and the many. The object perceived is presented as one whole, in which a variety of sense-elements is combined and interpreted. In simple sense-perception, however, there is no thought of such a relation as that of whole and parts. There is merely a synthesis of elements, in which this relation is implicit. This synthesis seems, moreover, to involve the element of activity in a new form. The sense-material is not simply passively received, but is combined by a certain constructive power, so as to form a unity or whole. Here again, however, the activity is not a conscious exercise of power. It is only by

---

ticular content that is asserted. There is thus at least an implicit complexity. But the meaning of this primitive assertion, as conceived by Mr. Hobhouse, is not quite clear to me.

subsequent reflection that we become aware that, in this phase of combination, or reference to the unity of an object, the mind has contributed something which is not directly present in the elements that are brought together. Activity, then, like the One and the Many, may be said to be implicit in the synthesis of sense-material.[1]

3. **The Presentation of a Definite Object.**   The synthesis of sense-material, so as to constitute a definite object, raises experience in general to a higher level.   The conscious being now has before him a group of things, held together in the unity of experience, and placed in various modes of relation and contrast.   In particular, such objects are distinguished from one another by the greater or less degree of closeness with which they are connected with the organic life of the conscious being that apprehends them.   In this distinction there lies the germ of the antithesis between the self and the not-self.[2]   But this antithesis is still only implicit at the level of simple perception.   An animal's limbs, or the other members of its species with which it is related in a group, are nearer to it than most other objects, and are more intimately connected with feeling.   This intimacy of connection gives rise to the various forms of animal emotion,[3] the nature of which it is not necessary here to discuss.   The

---

[1] According to such a view as that of Mr. Hobhouse, however, it is an implicit aspect which can never be explicitly separated off from the whole experience in which it is contained.

[2] See, on this point, Stout's *Manual of Psychology*, Book III., II., chap. ii.

[3] The personal or quasi-personal aspect of all emotion (even the coarsest forms of animal emotion) is a point that has perhaps not been adequately noticed by psychologists.   Emotion is a stirring up of the *whole* life of an organic being, and generally in relation to the life of some other.

actual modes of relationship of objects to one another, as well as the relation of them all to the subject by which they are apprehended, still remain implicit at this level of conscious development.

4. **The Recognition of Things.** More important, however, than any such relationships between different objects, is the fact that each object has at this stage of conscious life become a definite thing, capable of being apprehended in changing conditions. This implies the element of recognition in some form, and this again seems to involve some degree of ideal revival. Further, as soon as the recognition of an object as the *same* as one previously presented becomes possible, we have the germ of the consciousness of the universal, as the element of identity in the midst of difference. But all this can only be described as implicit at the level of simple perception. It is doubtful whether there is any actual ideal revival in the case of simple animal recognition, and probably the recognition of sameness means little more than that certain active tendencies are re-excited [1] Still, the fact of identity in difference is implied even in this.

5. **The Apprehension of Change.** Along with the recognition of more or less permanent objects, there arises also the apprehension of change. As Kant says, [2] it is only the permanent that changes. In a purely sensational experience, without any apprehension of permanent objects, there could be no consciousness of change; but as soon as anyone is aware of objects as abiding, it is possible also to watch their transformations. In the tracing of such transformations,

---

[1] See Stout's *Manual of Psychology*, Book III., I., chap. i., § 3.
[2] *Critique of Pure Reason*, Analogies of Experience.

there is involved the germ of the consciousness of the causal relation ; but this also can only be regarded as implicit.

6. **The Consciousness of Space and Time**.   In the apprehension of objects and their changes, relations of space and time are involved, though of course the thought of such relations is of much later development.   The distinct apprehension of an object requires the placing of it in certain definite relations to other objects around it ; and, on the other hand, all change implies time.   In movement, again, both space and time are involved.   Time is of course still more definitely present in such facts of experience as anticipation and recollection, but it may be doubted whether either of these is contained in the purely perceptual level of conscious life.[1]

7. **The Pursuit of Ends**.   If anticipation is not contained in this level of consciousness, there can of course be no definite pursuit of ends.   Yet the pursuit of ends must at least be regarded as implicit in perceptual experience. Indeed, it is probably the practical interest in objects that chiefly leads to that concentration of attention upon them by which they come to be recognised as permanent things. Here again the active element in perceptual experience becomes prominent.[2]

8. **The Metaphysical Significance of Perception.**   It appears from this brief survey that all the elements that come out in Perception as having metaphysical importance

[1] The extent to which ideal elements are involved in the perceptual consciousness is a very difficult problem.   Possibly Stout, in his *Manual of Psychology*, is disposed to exclude them somewhat too rigorously.

[2] See, on this point, Stout's *Manual of Psychology*, Book III., I., chap. i., § 3.

are rather implicit than explicit.[1] Still, it seems worth while to take note of the way in which they appear and operate at this level of consciousness. The chief elements are no doubt the apprehension of Things (containing in germ the ideas of Substance and Individuality), the apprehension of change (containing in germ the idea of causal sequence), the apprehension of the Spatial and Temporal (which must be carefully distinguished from the definite *thought* of Space and Time), and purposiveness in action (containing in germ the idea of End and Means). The full significance of all these elements, however, can only be seen in the more explicit form in which they present themselves at the conceptual level of experience.

---

[1] The meaning of this is that, when we are studying the perceptual level of experience, we must recognise these elements as working in it, but not working as factors of which the being itself is conscious. Thus, all conation may be said to imply an end ; but it does not imply the consciousness of an end. Similarly, the apprehension of objects and their changes involves space and time, but not the consciousness of these.

CHAPTER IV.

THOUGHT.

1. The Nature of Conceptual Experience. The conceptual level of consciousness is chiefly characterised by the explicit development of those elements that in perception are only implicit, i.e. the gradual *presentation* to consciousness of elements that at first only *work* in consciousness. The ideal revival of presented objects is one of the most important of these, on which perhaps all the others turn. It is this that makes possible the explicit recognition of objects as the same in the midst of change. It is this also that enables us to think of time as containing past, present, and future possibilities of experience. And it is this that makes the definite distinction of the permanent and the changing possible. Finally, it is through this that the presentation of ends is made explicit. Ideal revival in itself, however, would not suffice to lead to all these results. If it merely meant the presentation of images, these would carry us very little farther than the perception of particular objects. It is only in so far as we are enabled, by the help of images, to form universal conceptions, that we are definitely carried beyond the perceptual level, and that further advance is made possible. Accordingly, it is to the intro duction of this element of Universality in consciousness that we must now direct attention.

2. **Universals.**   The element of Universality may be said to be implicit even in the simplest sense-experience.[1]   Of no sensation can it be said merely *that* it is ; we may always inquire *what* it is ; and the "what" would always have to be expressed by some universal determinations.   If we call a colour blue or a pain intense, or a sound sharp, we are using certain characteristics which are general in their nature ; and without such characteristics it seems clear that there could be no sense-experience at all.   But of course it is reflection on sense-experience that reveals the universality of these determinations.   They are not recognised by sense itself as having a universal nature ; nor perhaps can they even be said to be used in sense-experience in a universal way.   With respect to the latter point, at least, there seems to be a distinct advance in perceptual experience.   Here objects are at least practically recognised as being of a certain kind.   When an animal recognises one of its own species, or one of a species that preys upon it, or that it preys upon, it is making use of the element of generality, however little it may be aware of the fact.   In all perceptual experience this practical use of the universal is prominent ; but it is probably true that at this level of consciousness there is still no apprehension of the universal as such.   It is in thought that the universal, as such, is first clearly brought forward.   Indeed it may fairly be said that the explicit presence of the universal is the fundamental point by which

---

[1] What Stout says about the 'acquirement of meaning' is a great help to the understanding of this. See his *Manual of Psychology*, Book I., chap. ii., § 9.

thought-experience is characterised.   Hence it is important to understand fully what is involved in this element.   Some consideration of the nature of generalisation may help to make this clear.

3. **Generalisation**.   It is probably well to begin by notic-ing a view of generalisation which has had a great deal of vogue in modern times, especially among British philo-sophers, and which has been to a considerable extent misleading.   I refer to the view which connects it with the process of abstraction.   We are supposed, according to this view, to begin with a number of complex individual objects, and gradually to discover points that they have in common, by the omission of those in which they disagree.   In this way, it is thought, we advance from the individual to the general, and from the less general to the more general. This view has, of course, a good deal of plausibility, and even an element of truth; but the difficulties that are involved in it may be well seen by tracing its influence through the successive positions of Locke, Berkeley, and Hume.   Locke's account [1] of the formation of general ideas, though not very definite in its statements, seems to imply that we arrive at them simply by leaving out the pecu-liarities of individual things, or of the smaller classes that lead up to the more general conceptions.   Thus we get at the general idea of triangle, by leaving out all particulars with regard to the size of its angles, the length of its sides, and the other special determinations that distinguish one triangle from another.   Against this view Berkeley urged [2]

---

[1] *Essay concerning Human Understanding*, Book III., chap. iii., §§ 6-9, and Book IV., chap. vii., § 9.

[2] *Principles of Human Knowledge*, Introduction, §§ 11-24.

that, if such a process were carried out, nothing would be left to set before the mind at all. Hume, following up the same line of thought, was led to the conclusion[1] that the general name is all that is really before our minds when we think of a class of things; and that the generality of the name simply means its power of calling up, when required, an indefinite number of particular images. Thus the view that general ideas are formed simply by abstraction leads naturally to the view that, properly speaking, general ideas are not formed at all.[2]

Further reflection on this view of generalisation may serve to convince us that it is applicable (if at all) only in the least important and significant cases—those that are furthest removed from real generality of thought. Such a general idea as that of 'red things' may fairly be said to be formed by simple abstraction. If we simply want to call attention to the fact that an object is red, it does not matter in the least whether it is a rose or a nose, a fire or a robin's breast. We are interested in the purely sensuous fact of colour. Or again, if we make a general class of words beginning with the letter A, we may leave out every other peculiarity by which any such words are distinguished. If, then, all general ideas were like the idea of red or A, such a theory of generalisation might possibly be accepted as true and sufficient.[3] But such general ideas can hardly be called

---

[1] *Treatise of Human Nature*, Book I., Part I., § 7.

[2] Hume, almost always more acute and more candid than his followers, was well aware that the acceptance of this view involved the practical use of general names in impenetrable mystery. See *Treatise on Human Nature*, as above.

[3] Even in these cases the view is not strictly accurate; but we need not insist on that point here.

thoughts at all : and, when we pass from such simple instances, it seems clear that the theory will no longer work. The general idea of colour is not got by leaving out the special features of red, blue, green, purple, etc. If we did this, nothing would be left. So also, if we formed the idea of animal by leaving out all the special features of the oyster, the whale, the elephant, the kangaroo, etc., there would be no content left in the idea at all. In such instances it seems clear that the general conception is formed rather by *concretion* than by abstraction. Colour means the system within which red, blue, green, and purple have their place, rather than a residuum from which they are all omitted: So too the general conception of animals is the thought of an ideal whole in which oyster, whale, elephant, kangaroo, etc., all have their proper places, rather than some empty abstraction from which the peculiarities of all these are excluded. This is, perhaps, still more apparent when we take such a conception as that of Art or Religion.[1] In short, the more completely the element of thought enters in, the less true is it to say that our conception is merely abstract.[2]

Viewed in this way, the process by which the general conception is formed appears to be simply a further extension of the process by which the perception of an individual object is put together. Even there, indeed, as we have already noted, the element of generality enters in. An object of any considerable complexity can be held together as an individual whole only by a continuous

---

[1] See below, Book III., chap. v., § 4.

[2] See on this point Lotze's *Logic*, Book I., chap. i., § 23. Cf. also Dr. Bosanquet's *Essentials of Logic*, pp. 95-7. Hegel's Essay, " Who is the abstract Thinker ? " (*Wer denkt abstrakt* ?), is very instructive on this point. See Wallace's *Logic of Hegel*, Prolegomena, chap. xxi.

synthesis in which past experience is used in connection with present impressions. The sameness of past with present in this continuous synthesis involves the same element of identity in difference which operates in the synthesis of diverse objects as members of a common class. In both cases an ideal whole is used for the synthesis of a manifold content. The difference lies mainly in the relative degree of definiteness with which the manifold is distinguished from the unity in which it is brought together. In the simple perception of an individual object there is no such distinction. In the definite thought of a class the distinction is sharply drawn. The mere thought of a general concept (such as triangle, religion, etc.), not regarded definitely as a class, lies midway between these two extremes.

If this view of generalisation is correct, it would seem that the element of identity in difference is what is chiefly important. Accordingly, this element now claims some further attention.

4. **The Meaning of Identity**. The importance of a true theory of identity has been emphasised by several recent writers.[1] The danger lies chiefly in separating the element of sameness from that of difference. When we are dealing with words that begin with A, we are apt to say that in all cases the initial letter is the same, while in other respects the words are different. But, even in so simple an example as this, the A with which different words begin cannot be the same without any difference. But in such a case

---

[1] See especially Dr. Bosanquet's Essay *On the Philosophical Import-ance of a true Theory of Identity* in *Mind*, Old Series, Vol. XIII., p. 356 (reprinted in *Essays and Addresses*).

the difference can be so readily overlooked that we are apt to treat it as non-existent. In more complex cases, however, we become somewhat puzzled. Is the beauty of a statue, for instance, the same thing as the beauty of a landscape? Is the element of Religion in Fetichism the same as it is in Christianity? Is the goodness of a stone wall the same as that of a heroic action? It was such questions as this that led to the formulation of Plato's doctrine of Ideas or Types. The eternal Form, he maintained, is the same in such cases, though the particular manifestation varies; and it may be supposed to exist apart from these manifestations. But this is a somewhat naïve way of evading the difficulty.[1] The truth seems rather to be that there is no such thing as mere sameness, but that the element of identity always appears in the midst of difference. In colour, for instance, it is not the case that there is some one thing present in red, blue, green, etc., which can be separated from all these, and is the same in each. The truth is rather that these various colours form a continuous scale, and that the single term "colour" is used to express the fact of their combination in this connected system. So also it is with animal life, religion, art, government, goodness, and all other conceptions that have a genuine universality. What we have in all of them is the combination of a manifold material within a more or less systematic form. It is

---

[1] According to some (especially Dr. Henry Jackson and Mr. Archer-Hind) Plato himself got beyond this position in the end, and postulated universal Types only in the case of real kinds—these Types being further regarded as exemplars, rather than as common elements. But this view of the development of Plato's Ideal Theory is still open to doubt.

such identity in the midst of difference that constitutes the essential characteristic of our concrete concepts—an identity which is very real, but which cannot be separated out from the differences in connection with which it occurs.

5. **The Concrete Concept**. The Concept, in the proper sense of the term, seems to be more concrete than the percept, just as the latter is more concrete than the simple sensation. What chiefly tends to prevent us from seeing this is the fact that, while it is more concrete, it is also more schematic. In the case of the simple sensation there is no distinction between what it is and what it means for us ; but the more we advance in the development of experience, the more pronounced does this distinction become. Even the perception of an individual object is to a certain extent schematic ; it is an outline that is only partly filled in. The more complex the object is, the truer does this become ; and in the case of the concept it becomes so apparent as almost to obscure the other aspects of the process. The concept is always to some extent an ideal ; it aims at being more than is actually realised in it. Hence it always tends to be in the making rather than an accomplished product. We cannot understand its full significance without taking note of the processes of judgment and reasoning in which it is built up, and by which its content is unfolded.[1]

6. **Judgment**. The study of the growth of the judgment belongs to psychology, and the analysis of its forms belongs to logic. Here we are only concerned with its essential

---

[1] The significance of the Concept is well brought out by Professor Muirhead in a paper in *Mind*, New Series, Vol. V., p. 508.

significance. Now, the first significance of the judgment
seems to lie in its being the mode in which the 'that' is
brought under the 'what.' It presents itself as the answer
to the question—What is that? [1] It is the process, that is
to say, in which the individual object is made definite by
means of universal determinations, or in which the percept is
brought within the scope of the concept. From this point
of view, judgment may be said to presuppose the concept.
But this process is at the same time that by which the
concept itself is determined. When we are able to say of
Fetichism, that it is a form of religion, we are at the same
time making possible for ourselves a more definite conception of what religion is. And so it comes about that,
while the judgment is at first the mode in which the percept
is brought under the concept, it ends by being the mode in
which the meaning of the concept is unfolded. When we
say, Fetichism is a form of religion, the question at once
presents itself, Why is it to be included in that particular
system? The answer is, Because it has such and such
characteristics, which constitute the essence of that particular system. In giving this answer, we are at once unfolding
the meaning of the concept, and at the same time giving the
ground for the inclusion of the percept, or of the smaller
concept, within it. And thus we are led on from Judgment
to Reasoning.

7. **Reasoning**. Reasoning arises from the attempt to find
the ground for a judgment. It seeks to answer the question
Why? as the judgment answers the question What? From
a psychological point of view, it probably owes its origin
primarily to doubt. The sight of a plant may suggest the

---

[1] See Stout's *Analytic Psychology*, Book II., chap. viii.

two judgments, "This is food" and "This is poison"; and
we are left in doubt which of them to adopt. Then we
begin to reason. We say, "It is food if its leaf is shaped in
a particular way, or if it has a certain smell." Or we say, "It
is food; for I saw some one eat a portion of it and suffer no
evil consequences." The assignment of the ground or condition removes the doubt, and at the same time enables us
to understand more clearly the relation between the particular percept and the concept by which it is determined.
The general tendency of this process is to lead us up from
the individual judgment—e.g. "This is food"—to the
universal judgment—e.g. "What has such and such characteristics is food." The result of this is to remove the
indefiniteness of the concept. Food gradually ceases to
mean a vague group of things that can be eaten, and comes
to mean things that have certain qualities with reference to
the support of life, and that can be distinguished by the
possession of certain characteristics. In logical language, it
comes to have a definite connotation or intensive meaning.[1]

8. **The Categories.** This at once raises the question—
What are the ways in which the meaning of concepts can
be determined? Aristotle's list of categories seems to have
been the first definite attempt to answer this question; and
on the whole this has been the essential meaning of subsequent attempts to enumerate the categories. When we
seek to give determinateness to our thoughts of things, we
use such modes of determination as are expressed by the
terms Quantity, Quality, Degree; or, again, we relate them to
other things by such determinations as position in Space and

---

[1] On the Judgment and its forms, see Bosanquet's *Logic*, Vol. I.,
Book I. ; Hobhouse's *Theory of Knowledge*, Part I., chaps. ix.-xi., etc.

Time, Cause, and the like. If we had a complete list of such general conceptions, and saw their exact relations to one another, we should have a full understanding of what is meant by thought-determination. Accordingly, the effort to evolve the categories has been one of the greatest problems of recent philosophy.

9. **Method of finding the Categories.** Kant was the first who made a really systematic attempt to discover the categories ; and his method, as is well known, was to seek a clue for them in the forms of judgment. He also discovered what he called Ideas of Reason (which are also a species of category) by an examination of the forms of reasoning ; while, again, a survey of the practical use of reason and of the aesthetic and teleological judgments yielded some further modes of determination. The subsequent course of philosophical thought has made it pretty apparent that Kant's method, bold and suggestive though it is, is essentially futile. He can get the categories from the forms of judgment only by interpreting the judgment in a way which he himself shows to be a mistaken one ; and even then his transition from the forms of judgment to the categories that are to be derived from them is artificial and unconvincing.[1]

The most remarkable attempt to discover the categories, since the time of Kant, is undoubtedly that of Hegel. The method that he uses, as we have already noted, is that of Dialectic. He contends that, if we start with the simplest determination—that of mere Being—we are forced, by the inner incoherence of such a conception, to advance to further and more concrete determinations ; and that in this way all the thought-determinations may be evolved from the

---

[1] See Caird's *Critical Philosophy of Kant*, Book I., chap. iii.

F

simplest of them. It is doubtful, however, whether this is really possible without a certain amount of sophistry. No doubt it is possible to arrange the fundamental conceptions in order of relative simplicity, and it is then comparatively easy to see that the more complex supply what is wanting in the more simple ; but it hardly seems that the order is a linear one, or that the mode of transition from one to another can be regarded as always of the same kind.[1] The Hegelian arrangement of the categories is perhaps in the end hardly less artificial than that of Kant.

A more hopeful method would perhaps be the more purely genetic one. We might note the various modes of determination as gradually arising in the development of experience, getting more and more definiteness as experience advances, and taking on new meanings as it becomes more complex. To some extent we have been indicating how this might be done. We have seen how such conceptions as those of Kind, Quality, Degree, and the like are involved even in the simplest sense-experience, how determinations of Space and Time are used in the perceptual consciousness, how the rudimentary ideas of Substance and Causation are gradually introduced, how it comes to be recognised that the idea of End is involved, and other conceptions of a similar nature. To put these in a definite order, however, and note the precise significance that they have at each stage of development, would be a herculean task, and one far beyond the scope of such an outline as this. It must suffice for our purpose at present merely to hint at the possibility of such a method of exposition.

---

[1] See M'Taggart's *Studies in the Hegelian Dialectic*, pp. 121-134. Cf. also above, Book I., chap. iv., § 5.

10. **The Significance of the Categories.** The full significance of the categories could not be properly discussed without
a complete exhibition of the place occupied by each of them
in the building up of our knowledge—a task that is far
beyond the scope of our present inquiry. But, apart from
such a detailed investigation, we may note some general
points with regard to the categories that may help to make
their significance clear to us.

The categories are all essentially, as Kant contended,
modes of unity. They are the ways in which the manifold
content of our experience is gradually reduced to systematic
order. Number, for instance, is such a mode. This mode
is applicable to any content that can be regarded as containing discrete elements or units, and enables us to compare
any elements in our experience that are in other respects
homogeneous. Quality is another mode of bringing certain
elements of experience into systematic relation to one another.
Again, elements that are the same in quality may be brought
into relation to one another by the category of Degree.
Causation, again—however it may be finally interpreted—
enables us to connect heterogeneous objects as uniformly
accompanying one another, or as connected by the relation
of ground and consequent. Time and Space, in like manner,
are forms in which all the objects of our experience are
placed, and by means of which they are systematically
related to one another. The idea of End is another such
mode of systematic connection. All of these, then, have
this in common, that they are the modes in which
systematic unity is interwoven into the world of our
experience.

When, however, we thus view the categories as modes of
unity in our experience, a further point soon discloses itself

with regard to them, viz., that the system which they thus
introduce is an incomplete system.   In some cases this incompleteness makes itself apparent by the discovery of an
arbitrary limit, in other cases by the impossibility of reaching any end.   The latter cases are no doubt the more
interesting and striking.   The case of Causation is one of
the most obvious.   Here an event is brought into the
systematic order of experience by being connected with
some other event that uniformly precedes it, or that may in
some way be regarded as its ground.   The latter event,
however, makes a similar demand to be brought into the
systematic order of experience by connection with some
other antecedent or ground, and so on indefinitely.   Such a
mode of systematic connection could never be completed
unless we could suppose, either that at some point we came
upon an event which was of such a peculiar nature as to
make no further demand to be brought into the system, or
that we go round in a circle which in the end is closed.   A
similar difficulty presents itself with regard to the systems of
Space and Time.   Kant's discussion of the Antinomies may
be referred to in connection with these.[1]   The general
difficulty in both cases is that any ultimate limitation of
the world within these forms can be thought of only by
supposing another world outside of ours, by which it is
limited—unless, indeed, Time and Space could be thought
of as returning into themselves, as if in a circle, and the
existence of the world in them as a recurrent cycle.[2]   On the

---

[1] *Critique of Pure Reason*, " Transcendental Analytic."

[2] The recognition of such a cycle would of course be subversive of
the ordinary conceptions of Time, Space, and Causation. It would
involve, for instance, with regard to Time, that any event that comes
after another might with equal truth be said to come before it.

other hand, in the use of such conceptions as Number, Quality, and Degree, we seem to be confronted with arbitrary limits—with limits, that is to say, which are determined, not by the nature of the system that we are applying, but by the nature of the material to which we apply it. The colours, for instance, seem to have a limited number of qualities and degrees.[1] So also there are a limited number of kinds of sensation. The incompleteness in such cases lies simply in the fact that the systematic mode of connection with which we are dealing seems to contain no ground within itself for the limitation of its material.

Without considering in detail the way in which this incompleteness shows itself in the case of the various categories, we may sum up the general fact by saying that it is the nature of all the categories to present Ideals to our minds. They all put before us forms of unity that seem to stretch beyond the particular content that is brought within them. In some cases this may seem to mean nothing more than that there are arbitrary limits to the materials with which we have to deal. In other cases it seems more definitely to imply that the mode of unity that we are using is not one that admits of completeness. It is the latter fact that leads to the dialectical treatment of the categories. If any of them are incapable of completeness, we may be led by this fact to seek for others, in which the elements of completeness can be supplied. Without, however, considering for the present the possibility of such a process, it seems desirable at this point to give some further attention to the meaning of such ideals in consciousness.

11. **Ideals in Thought.** The inevitable suggestion of

---

[1] See Titchener's *Outline of Psychology*, p. 48.

Ideals by the process of conception is perhaps nowhere better brought out than in the writings of Plato. The thought of a thing—as distinguished from the sensuous apprehension of it—becomes with him its Form or Type; and this is at the same time conceived by him as the Ideal to which it points. The world for thought is the world seen in the light of the Ideal of what is Best. The State scientifically conceived is the Ideal Republic. To put it in this way is, no doubt, to lay a somewhat extreme emphasis on the ideal aspect of conception. Yet it is characteristic of all conceptual apprehension that it sets up an Ideal. Mere sensation points to nothing beyond itself. Even in perception the meaning does not much outrun the actual content. But even the simplest conception carries us into a world that is not realised; and, as the conceptual process advances, it sets us more and more upon the building up of systems for which the filling is very imperfectly present to us, until finally we are led into systems for which it even seems impossible that the necessary content could ever be found at all. It is such systems that Kant speaks of as Ideas of Reason, but perhaps he makes the antithesis too sharp between these and the ordinary categories. The transition seems to be a gradual one from those rudimentary conceptions which are little more than generic images—say, the conception of a plate—to those complex conceptions which carry us completely away from the objects that are presented to us in sense experience. The great problem then comes to be to determine how far the process that thus carries us to the construction of systems for which there is no actual content, is to be regarded as a valid one. And this is really the most fundamental problem of Metaphysics. But before we pass to the consideration of this, we must notice some further points with regard to the working of the ideal element in the conceptual level of consciousness.

12. **Ideals in Feeling.** We should have but a very imperfect apprehension of the working of the ideal element at the conceptual level if we thought of it only as a purely intellectual form. It must be considered also in connection with feeling. Now, it seems probable that at all levels of conscious development feeling may be best understood as a certain apprehension of harmony or want of harmony between some particular content and the form of unity within which it is brought. At the sensational level the mode of unity is constituted by the general organic life of the individual or by the vitality of some particular organ. At the perceptual level this is supplemented by the unity of the objects that are presented to us, and in particular by the ends that are more or less consciously set up. At the intellectual level, however, the chief forms of unity are of the nature of intellectual systems. The fitting of a particular content harmoniously within a certain systematic form yields intellectual satisfaction. Now this fact provides a powerful stimulus to the creation of such systematic forms and to the attempt to bring particular contents within them ; and this is partly the reason why the mind tends to outrun its positive material in the construction of intellectual systems. This is a point that has to be carefully borne in mind when we are considering the validity of such constructions. The everlasting quarrel between poetry and philosophy, of which Plato speaks, depends largely on this. Poetry—the constructive imagination —is continually forming ideal systems and bringing material within them or creating material to fill them ; and if such systems are based simply on the demands of feeling,

intellectual criticism is not able to regard them as valid. But it is seldom the case that such constructions can be said to rest *merely* on feeling. The demand of feeling is in general at the same time a demand for intellectual completeness. This we shall have to consider more fully in the sequel.[1]

13. **Ideals in Action.** On the active side of consciousness also the working of the ideal makes its influence felt. The activities of a purely animal being are guided by inherited instincts or by adjustment to present surroundings. It is only thinking beings that are capable of guiding themselves by the definite idea of ends. Such ends involve the presentation of something unrealised, which is regarded as better than what is actually present in experience. With the growth of thought such ends take more and more complex forms, until finally some attempt is made to formulate a *summum bonum*, a supreme good in which all the demands of our nature should find satisfaction. Here again the question arises how far such a practical ideal is a valid object of thought.

14. **The Metaphysical Significance of Thought.** The foregoing remarks may perhaps suffice to bring before us the leading elements that are at work in the conceptual level of conscious development. And it is not difficult to see where the metaphysical problem lies with respect to these. We see that the essential feature of the conceptual process lies in its bringing the complex material of experience into the unity of wider and wider systematic forms. This is no doubt a process that is begun even in perception ; but perception rests content with the simple

---

[1] See especially Book III., chap. iv.

construction of objects, or at the utmost with the apprehension of their most elementary spatial and temporal
relations. With the growth of conception, far larger constructions are attempted—constructions that often seem to
point to ends of which no possible actualisation is discoverable. Now the problem arises, with regard to such
constructions, how far they can be regarded as valid. It
seems clear that, in discussing such a question, we cannot
apply any standard outside of experience itself. The
question, in fact, can only mean, how far the attempt
to introduce systematic unity into experience can finally
be made to work; and perhaps this is a question that
could only be finally answered if the process of systematisation had been carried to its utmost possible extent.
Still, apart from this, it may at least be possible to find
some provisional answer or approximation to an answer.
Of course it may be said that a similar problem arises
even with reference to the simple constructions that are
involved in sense-perception. Even there we come in
time to regard some modes of construction as illusory;
and this is a kind of criticism at which even animals seem
to be in some degree capable of arriving, at least in a
practical way. The criticism which thought is capable
of passing on its own constructions is, however, of a much
more extensive and fundamental nature. Such criticism
is the essential work of Metaphysics.

The advantage of rising to this problem, as we have now
done, through a genetic study, lies mainly in the fact that
it enables us to put the whole of our material before ourselves in proper perspective. If we had simply started
with thought as criticising its own constructions, we should
have been in some danger of placing thought in undue

isolation from the other aspects of our conscious experience.[1]
It is best to study it, not as something that stands apart
by itself, but as the culminating point in the general
process of experience. Having now gone through this
genetic study, however, we are in a position to get a clearer
view of the situation by taking a general survey of the
results to which we have been led. We may thus prepare
the way for the final discussion of the value of these
thought-constructions.

---

[1] I think this is a defect that may to some extent be noted even in
such a work as Bradley's *Appearance and Reality*. The activity of
thought tends to be represented there as a sort of game in which we
happen to be engaged. From this point of view, Metaphysics comes
to be regarded almost as a whim of the individual· thinker—a way of
seeking satisfaction for the 'mystical side of our nature,' rather than an
intellectual necessity.

CHAPTER V.

RESULTS OF THE GENETIC SURVEY.

1. **General Nature of Experience re-considered.** The advantage of such a survey as we have now made lies chiefly in the fact that it enables us to have definitely before our minds a connected view of experience as a concrete whole, and so to see at least where the essential problem of Metaphysics really lies. In particular, it enables us to see more clearly the true meaning of that fundamental antithesis in experience on which, as we have seen, metaphysical speculation has mainly turned. In the survey of metaphysical theories given in an earlier chapter, we saw that most of the leading points of view, at least in modern times, were dependent on the recognition of an ultimate opposition between mind and matter, and that this opposition again is dependent in the end upon that between the world that is presented in consciousness and the self to which it is presented. We have seen that Dualism arises from the simple acceptance of this antithesis as an ultimate fact, that Idealism and Materialism arise from attempts to overcome it, that Agnosticism represents the despair of any ultimate solution of the problem that is involved in it, and that most other forms of metaphysical speculation are due to efforts of

a more or less complex kind to get finally beyond it. Now, we have not as yet arrived at any results that can be said to yield definite foundations for a metaphysical theory; but even such a survey as we have now made may suffice to abolish the fundamental antithesis to which we have referred, at least in the form in which it at first presents itself, and to substitute a somewhat different one for it. For we now see that the world of matter and the world of mind, in the only sense in which these two can be set in opposition to one another, are both ideal constructions; and, from the point of view that we have now reached, they both stand in opposition to the raw material which is brought within such ideal systems. Thus the Cartesian antithesis between matter and mind gives place to the Kantian between thought and sense. But even this latter opposition can no longer be regarded as a sharp and final one.[1] For the survey that we have made enables us to see that the process upwards from the raw material of sense to such complicated ideal constructions is a long and gradual one, and that it is impossible to point to any form or grade of experience in which these two aspects are not present in the most intimate connection with one another. From this point of view, therefore, experience is much more of a piece than it is apt at first to appear; and the problem of Metaphysics can no longer present itself as that of dealing with two opposing forms of reality, but rather as that of seeing how far it is possible to view the whole content of experience as a systematic unity. It seems clear that any solution

---

[1] The most fatal defect in Mr. M'Taggart's recent attempt to rehabilitate the Hegelian philosophy seems to me to lie in his revival of this Kantian antithesis. Cf. Baillie's *Origin and Significance of Hegel's Logic*, p. 357.

of the metaphysical problem which took the form of the assertion, that the ultimate reality is matter, or that the ultimate reality is mind,[1] or that the ultimate reality consists of some combination of matter and mind, or of something underlying both, would be an utterly unsatisfactory and utterly crude kind of solution. For it would leave the most fundamental problem untouched, that of really understanding what mind and matter mean for us. What we have to do is rather to take these as elements in the totality of our experience, and to try to see what place belongs to each within the concrete system of our world. They are not themselves terms that can be used in any ultimate solution of the universe, but rather names for certain aspects of that reality which it is our business to try to understand. To reach any such understanding, we must carefully note the various elements of which our experience is composed, and consider each of them in its relations to the whole. This is what such a genetic survey as we have given ought now to put us in a position to do. Having, then, traced the chief elements as they appear in the building up of our experience, we may now sum up the results to which we seem to be led, and so give a more definite form to the problems that still remain before us.

2. **The Elements of Experience.** It would appear from the survey that we have made, that the most fundamental antithesis in experience is that between the particular and the universal—as some recent writers have expressed

---

[1] In the sense in which mind, as the pure subject, is contrasted with matter. In another sense, as really including matter, mind may be the ultimate reality. In this more concrete sense, in which the content of experience is included, it has been a common practice to use the word 'spirit' rather than 'mind.'

it, that between the 'That' and the 'What,'[1] or, in the language of ancient Greek Philosophy, that between 'Matter' and 'Form.'[2] But, while this fundamental antithesis is to be recognised, it would appear also that at no point in our experience can it be said that we are presented either with pure Matter or with pure Form, either with a mere 'That,' or with a mere 'What.' Even the simplest sensation has some determination, and, on the other hand, every determination is the determination of a certain material. We seem able to say, however, that the development of experience proceeds on the whole from the less determinate to the more determinate, by the introduction of more and more definite constructive forms. The chief of these constructive forms would seem to be (1) those that appear even in simple sense-presentation, giving us those determinations by which we are able to discriminate Kinds, Qualities, and Degrees ; (2) those relations of Space and Time by which the objects of perception are placed in relation to one another ; (3) those more purely conceptual relations by which the objects that we think about are determined, e.g. those that are expressed by such terms as Substance and Accident. Cause and Effect, Number, Development, and the like ; (4) relations dependent on feeling and activity, such as those that contain the idea of Value and End. The problem of Metaphysics, as it now presents itself to us, is to understand these various modes of determination, and to see within what limits each is valid. Some further remarks on the chief levels

---

[1] See Bradley's *Appearance and Reality*, pp. 162 *sqq.*

[2] Of course these three antitheses are not exactly the same ; but they seem in the end to involve the same contrast.

of our experience may help to put this problem in a somewhat clearer light.

3. **The Sense-material.** The raw material that we find in sensation is the nearest approach that we can make in our experience to the purely undetermined and simply given. There is here hardly any form and hardly any construction. Yet it is clear that even this simple material is not a mere 'that,' not an absolutely πρώτη ὕλη. If it had not a certain determinateness, it would be nothing for our conscious experience at all. But its Form or What-ness is as far as possible removed from the character of intellectual determination. It is not a way in which we think about the material, but simply the way in which it comes to us. Hence it presents itself also as something quite inexplicable; we can say nothing more about it than that it is so. For this reason J. S. Mill was led, as we have seen, to affirm that the elementary differences of kind among sensations point to the ultimate limits of possible explanation. It might seem, then, that here at least the task even of the most resolute of metaphysicians must be simply that of chronicling what we find and passing on. But the speculative mind can hardly reconcile itself to this. It will still cherish the hope that some account might be given even of those most rudimentary forms, some ground for their appearing in one way rather than in another. We may at least say, however, that the hope of any such explanation is the most remote of all the dreams of specula-tion. Practically we have to accept the material of sensation as we find it, and confine ourselves to the consideration of the constructive forms within which it is afterwards brought.

4. **The World of Perception.** The world as we perceive it, on the other hand, is characterised by the presence of

constructive activity. This activity, however, is still of a comparatively limited and unintellectual kind. It is chiefly remarkable for the two great forms of Space and Time within which its objects are placed. These forms, as used in Perception, must of course be distinguished from Space and Time as we think them. As forms of perception, they have some degree of the same unintelligibility that belongs to the forms of simple sense-apprehension. If we ask, for instance, why space presents itself in three dimensions, and not in more, it seems almost as hopeless[1] to find any answer as when we try to find an explanation of the difference between a sound and a colour. Reflection, however, seems to show that the hopelessness in this case is not so extreme. It is at least possible to give a clear formulation of the problem, whereas in the case of mere sense-experience it would be almost as difficult to state definitely what is to be explained as to find an explanation —the difficulty lying in the fact that the objects to be dealt with are objects that can only be sensed, and cannot really be stated in terms of thought. Space and Time, then, give rise to intellectual problems that can be definitely set before us, and that may be regarded as the first problems of intellectual construction. Among such problems, the Antinomies that have been so fully discussed by Kant are no doubt the most striking.

5. **The World of Science.** As soon as we begin to think about our world, however, instead of simply perceiving

---

[1] Perhaps not quite as hopeless, for it seems conceivable that the three dimensions of space might be shown to be essential to the apprehension of an object as external. But it would be impossible to enter into the discussion of a problem of this kind in such a work as the present.

it, new constructive forms are introduced. We begin to use such ideas as those of Substance, Cause, Number, Force, Development, and the like ; and it is the work of the various sciences to seek, by means of such ideas, to make our world into a connected and coherent system. In this construction all the forms that are used are of an intellectual character, and an explanation tends to be sought for every use that is made of them. This effort after explanation soon comes to extend itself beyond the sphere within which such conceptions are at first applied. Thus, the use of causation in dealing with physical objects leads to its application also in connection with feelings and sensations. The forms of perception and of pure sense-experience, as well as the more intellectual modes of construction, demand scientific explanation ; and thus the world of science tends in the long run to be co-extensive with the universe.

6. **The Universe.** When, however, the sphere of science is thus extended, its character becomes gradually altered. If we are to understand the universe as a whole, we must have some fundamental principle, and some central point of view ; and the discussion of these leads us into philosophy, as distinguished from the particular sciences. Wider modes of construction are now involved. We cannot be satisfied, for instance, with the study of the relations of physical objects to one another, as causes and effects, but have to consider the relations of such objects to the unity of consciousness within which they are apprehended. And when attention is thus directed to the unity of consciousness, as well as to the particulur objects that are presented within it, the significance of feeling and activity begins to come into view ; and constructions are formed, in which the ideas of end and value play their part. We are led

G

into the consideration of the constructive activities that are shown in poetry, morality, and religion; and some attempt has to be made to determine the place of these also as elements in the constitution of the universe as a whole.

7. **The Problem of Metaphysics re-stated**. The problem of metaphysics, looked at in this way, is that of considering and criticising the whole work of that constructive activity which is involved in experience. It seeks to determine, we may say, how far such constructive activity can be carried, and what the final outcome of it is. In doing this, it has to note all the forms in which such activity appears, and then to ask how far each of them can be regarded as valid. It seems clear, however, on reflection, that there can be no other criterion of such validity than the possibility of working out successfully the line of activity that is involved. If any construction can really be made, it must be accepted as a valid one. For there is no test, outside of experience itself, by which experience can be judged. Accordingly, the question for Metaphysics may be put in this way—What are the fundamental forms of construction that are involved in the building up of our experience? How far is each of these forms coherent in itself and capable of being systematically worked out? This is the problem that we must set ourselves to consider in the following book. We cannot of course undertake to discuss it in such a work as this with any pretence at completeness or thoroughness of treatment. But even an imperfect sketch may be valuable in showing where some of the chief problems lie. We may take our general clue from the genetic survey that has already been given, and proceed to consider the following main modes of construction:

(1) **Perceptual Construction,** or that which is involved in the simple setting before us of a number of objects ;

(2) **Scientific Construction,** or that which is involved in the attempt to connect objects together, so as to think of them in relation to one another as parts of a larger system ;

(3) **Ethical Construction,** or that which is involved in the effort to bring objects into relation to a final end or good ;

(4) **Aesthetic Construction,** or that which is involved in the apprehension of objects in relation to feeling, as beautiful or the reverse ;

(5) **Religious Construction,** or that which is involved in the effort to view the universe as a complete system which is one, beautiful, and good ;

(6) **Speculative Construction,** or that which is involved in the systematic attempt to think out the justification for such a view of the universe.

This may not be a complete account of the modes of construction that are contained in our experience; and it may be also that there is some overlapping in those that are here enumerated. But there seems at least to be a certain broad distinction between them ; and they seem to contain among them all the leading forms of synthesis. We may hope, therefore, that the consideration of them will at least bring us face to face with all the most important problems. The order of our study will continue to be, as far as possible, the genetic one.

BOOK III. CRITICISM OF IDEAL CONSTRUCTIONS.

CHAPTER I.

PERCEPTUAL CONSTRUCTION.

1. **General Nature of Perceptual Construction.** The synthesis of sense-material in the construction of objects of perception takes place so simply and directly that one is in some danger of forgetting that any synthesis is involved at all. It seems at least as if the synthesis took place entirely on the initiation of the material itself. The possibility of illusions is the chief fact that serves to remind us that this is not entirely true. When we find that we have made a wrong construction, we can hardly ignore the fact that we have made a construction. The circumstance, however, that even the lower animals can make such constructions, both correctly and incorrectly, shows how little conscious activity is involved in them. For this very reason it is difficult to entertain any serious doubts with regard to the validity of such constructions. What comes of itself seems to carry its own authority with it. But the fact of illusions again helps us to realise the possibility and legitimacy of such doubts in particular cases. Of one thing, however, it is hardly possible to

entertain any serious doubt, viz., that by perceptual construction it is possible to put together a coherent arrangement of objects which will stand and work sufficiently
well for all the practical purposes of life.[1] Doubt may
legitimately enter in only when we reflect upon the arrangement of objects thus put together, and ask whether it
is capable of being made into a coherent universe, or
whether it can be viewed as a partial aspect of such a
universe, or whether it must in the end be described, in
the language of Mr. Bradley, as nothing better than
'useful nonsense.' To answer this question it is necessary
to consider more in detail the nature of the construction
that is made in the perceptual consciousness.

2. **The Synthesis of Simple Apprehension.** Every real
perception of objects involves something of the nature
of apperception. The details of the sense-material are
somehow brought to unity in virtue of some connecting
principles, which may be more or less clearly apprehended.
In the simplest constructions of the purely animal consciousness no doubt such connecting principles may be supplied
by the presence of practical needs and the formation of
psycho-physical dispositions on the basis of these.[2] In
such simple constructions the difficulties contained in the
use of general principles remain implicit. Achilles can
pass the tortoise in spite of Zeno ; and the bird can hatch
its young without being troubled by the problem how

---

[1] Hence Descartes urged that doubt is as much out of place in action
as it is all-important in speculation. Scepticism seldom extends itself
to practical life. Hence the futility of practical refutations of scepticism,
like that of Reid against Hume.

[2] See Stout's *Manual of Psychology*, Book I., chap. ii., § 13, and
Analytic Psychology, Vol. I., pp. 21-24.

anything can become what it is not. Such actions, and the modes of apprehension that are implied in them, seem simple and direct to the consciousness in which they take their rise. It is only to the reflective consciousness that looks on and tries to understand them that they present problems and mysteries.

3. **The Synthesis of Recognition.** It is possible that in these purely practical perceptions there is no object present to consciousness that is not also present to sense— memory and anticipation being only practically or implicitly, and not consciously or explicitly, involved. But the slightest advance beyond this leads to some more or less definite recognition of an object as having a past, a present, and a future. This also, no doubt, is a mode of construction that may be carried on without any consciousness of the problems that are contained in it. But somewhat less reflection is necessary to bring them out. The object that is thus recognised is in some way apprehended as the *same* whenever it presents itself; and the mere liability to error in this synthesis suffices to some extent to call attention to the magnitude of the step that is thus taken. Identity among changing conditions is seldom—perhaps we may say never—even for practical purposes, a pure identity; and very little reflection is required to throw doubt upon its reality. The doctrine of the Heraclitean flux, and the scepticism about universals [1] that accompanies it, belong to a comparatively early phase of reflective thought. It requires, no doubt, a somewhat more subtle reflection to see that the recognition of past forms of con-

---

[1] Expressed in the saying—" We cannot step into the same river twice."

scious experience involves either, as Mr. Bradley puts it,[1] some doctrine of a resurrection of the body or else the realisation that real universals operate in our consciousness, and that our experience does not consist of separate units.[2] But, as soon as we realise this, the apparent simplicity of the perceptual consciousness is broken down, and we are face to face with the most difficult intellectual problems. The question is at once forced upon us—What are the elements of identity in our conscious experience by which the diverse content of our particular presentations is held together, so as to be capable of the synthesis that is involved in recognition ?

4. **The Consciousness of Kind.** The practical recognition of objects seems to depend primarily on sameness of kind. The recognition of animals by one another is probably to a large extent generic, and consists for the most part in the suggestion of appropriate movements.[3] The cat knows the dog chiefly as something to be avoided ; and the dog knows the cat chiefly as something to be chased. Such knowledge contains the germ of the apprehension of things as falling into different kinds. And when such consciousness of kind is traced back to its most rudimentary elements, we come upon the differences of kind in our primitive sense-experiences. A taste is one thing, a colour another, a sound another ; and we do not seem to be able to get behind such ultimate distinctions to any ground by which they can be explained. For this very reason, no particular difficulty presents itself with regard to

---

[1] *Principles of Logic*, Book II., Part II., chap. i.

[2] Cf. Stout's *Analytic Psychology*, Vol. I., pp. 273 *sqq.*

[3] See Stout's *Manual of Psychology*, Book III., chap. i., § 6.

differences of kind. Where there is nothing to be understood, there is nothing even to be asked; and where the mind has nothing to take hold of it finds nothing to complain of—no disturbing ἀκαταληψία. Such surds, however, such entirely irresolvable kinds, would seem at least to be very few in number; and the mind cannot easily find satisfaction in regarding anything as an ultimate surd. Even our purely perceptual determinations present in general something of the nature of systematic connections; and the connection that we thus find reflects itself back, so to speak, upon the ultimate kinds, and makes us dissatisfied with the apparent want of connection in them. A surd is apt to seem absurd. This is perhaps a prejudice; but it is a prejudice that seems inseparable from the nature of thought, which necessarily aims at transparent intelligibility.

5. **Distinctions of Quality.** Qualities of things, unlike ultimate kinds, are not, in the phrase of Anaxagoras, "cut off with a hatchet" from one another. The qualities of pure sensation, on which others depend, form continuous scales stretching between certain fixed points;[1] and this continuity gives them at least an air of greater intelligibility. The points, however, between which such scales stretch—e.g. white and black, or red and blue, in the colour continuum —present themselves in quite as arbitrary a way as the distinctions of ultimate kinds. We know what such differences mean, if nobody asks us; but as soon as a question is raised concerning them, it seems hopeless to attempt an answer.

---

[1] This seems to be true of the more highly developed senses—perhaps less so of the others, where the distinctions are less definitely qualitative, and rather more like differences of kind. See above, Book II., chap. ii., § 4.

With regard to the continuity of such scales, two points may be worth noting, as serving to throw some light on the nature of the system that is involved in it.

One is the problem of Hume,[1] "Suppose a person to have enjoyed his sight for thirty years, and to have become perfectly well acquainted with colours of all kinds, excepting one particular shade of blue, for instance, which it never has been his fortune to meet with. Let all the different shades of that colour, except that single one, be placed before him, descending gradually from the deepest to the lightest; 'tis plain that he will perceive a blank where that shade is wanting, and will be sensible, that there is a greater distance in that place betwixt the contiguous colours than in any other. Now I ask, whether 'tis possible for him, from his own imagination, to supply this deficiency, and raise up to himself the idea of that particular shade, as tho' it had been conveyed to him by his sense?" Hume answers, with characteristic candour,[2] "I believe there are few but will be of opinion that he can." It may be doubted whether this is the correct answer;[3] and also whether, under the conditions described, it is correct to say that the person would "perceive a blank." But the mere possibility of such questions is perhaps enough for our present purpose.

Another question, which connects itself at once with this one, is the following: Does the continuity of a qualitative scale imply an infinite possibility of intermediate grada-

---

[1] *Treatise of Human Nature*, Book I., Part I., sect. 1.

[2] For it is distinctly contrary to his own general theory, that no idea can be formed except as a simple copy of an impression. This he himself fully recognises; but apparently he thinks the contradiction unimportant.

[3] At least with reference to a 'single shade.' For a considerable portion of the colour scale it might be true.

tions, or can it be properly regarded, as Hume regards it,[1] as consisting of a finite number of points? Experience seems to show that there is a finite number of distinguishable shades in the colour scale.[2] If these are to be regarded as exhausting the possibilities of our colour experience[3] the differences do not after all merge in each other, and the intelligibility of the series is more apparent than real. It retains, in that case, something of the abruptness that is characteristic of difference of kind.

The consideration of these points may help us to see how little it is the case that such qualitative continua have the character of intelligible systems.

6. **Distinctions of Degree.** Degree comes somewhat nearer than Quality to complete intelligibility. It is not a continuous transition from one arbitrary point to another; but rather presents itself as a universal form of all sense experience, which must always be somewhere between zero and the complete occupation of the focus of consciousness. For this reason, Kant described it[4] as a characteristic that can be referred to all sense-perception by an *a priori* "anticipation"—thus violating the general principles of his philosophy[5]

---

[1] *Treatise of Human Nature*, Book I., Part II., sects. 1 and 2.

[2] See Titchener's *Outline of Psychology*, p. 48.

[3] This may not really be the case. The possibilities of difference are not necessarily as limited as the possibilities of discrimination.

[4] *Critique of Pure Reason*, " Anticipations of Perception."

[5] For he denies, in general, that the material element in our conscious experience, as distinguished from the formal element, can be determined *a priori*; and he does not regard Degree as one of the forms. Hence he describes this anticipation of sense-perception as a kind of uncovenanted grace. In reality the form under which we bring intensities would seem to have as much claim to be *a priori* as that under which we bring extensities and protensities.

for the sake of Degree, as Hume had already done for the sake of Quality. What we have to say, it would seem, is that all sense-experience presents itself to us as lying between a possible more and a possible less. This "more and less" points to an ultimate most and least; but both these limits are, so far as actual sense-experience is concerned, purely ideal. A zero in consciousness means simply absence of consciousness; and an absolute fulness, or complete occupation of the focus, would seem to be equally impossible in any positive experience.[1] Thus we appear, in this case, to escape from the arbitrary bounds that are involved in Quality, only to fall into the still greater difficulty of un-realisable limits. As regards any actual sense-experience that we can ever have, the Degree of a presentation would seem to be as arbitrary as its Quality or Kind.

7. **The Apprehension of Space.** Space is even more definitely and obviously of the nature of a universal form than Degree is. Here Kant had much less difficulty in maintaining the *a priori* character of the determination. And, so long as we accept it simply as a perceptual form, it does not appear to present any special problem. Its three-dimensional limitation does, indeed, prevent it from being completely intelligible, and gives it a more or less arbitrary character.[2] But it is chiefly when we pass beyond the

---

[1] It would come under the general ban of Hobbes—"*Idem semper sentire et non sentire ad idem recidunt.*" An experience which excluded every other would not be a definite experience at all. Cf. Ward's article on Psychology in the *Encyclopaedia Britannica*, p. 49.

[2] So also with the general distinction of regions and directions in space, the contrast between right and left hand gloves and screws, etc. See Kant's essay *On the Rational Basis for the Distinction of Regions in Space.* Cf. Caird's *Critical Philosophy of Kant*, Vol. I., p 166.

material of actual sense-perception, and try to think of the
world as a whole regarded as a system of parts in Space,
that the difficulties of this mode of construction become
apparent. These difficulties are somewhat similar in their
general nature to those that arise with respect to the limit-
ing conceptions implied in Degree; but they are more
serious with regard to Space, just on account of the greater
definiteness and universality of its form. We are not specially impelled, as a rule, to place one Degree in relation to
another; and so the problem of thinking out the complete
series of Degrees does not present itself as a pressing one.
But we do place the various objects of our experience
definitely in relation to one another in Space; and so we are
led to inquire to what this mode of determination ultimately
points. The difficulties involved in it are sufficiently brought
out by Kant in his discussion of the Antinomies, from which
we see that the world cannot be distinctly thought either as
limited or as unlimited within the form of Space. Hence
we cannot regard it as a form within which any finally
satisfactory and complete intellectual construction can be
made.

8. **The Apprehension of Time.** As a form of perceptual
experience, Time is even more universal than Space, though
practically both are involved in all real apprehension of
objects.[1] As it has no dimensions, but only a continuous
flow, it is free from the arbitrariness that seems to lie in the
three-dimensional character of space. On the other hand,
it suffers from the pure ideality of its determinations, only

---

[1] This was in the end brought out by Kant in the second edition of the
Critique of Pure Reason, General Note on the System of Principles in
the "Transcendental Analytic." Cf. Caird's *Critical Philosophy of Kant*,
Vol. I., chap. ix.

the present being capable of actual presentation in any given percept. This must not, however, be taken too strictly. Time is not discrete, and no actual experience is confined to a mere moment, any more than it is confined to a mere point in space.[1] But the chief difficulty in connection with Time, when it is taken as an object of reflection, is similar to that which presents itself in the case of Space, viz., the problem of ultimate limits. In the case of Time, this problem appears chiefly in the necessity of thinking of an absolute beginning. Kant has sufficiently brought out the Antinomies that are involved here, just as he has with regard to the boundaries of Space. And in this case also the only way out of the difficulty is to be found in recognising the essentially limited character of temporal determinations, i.e. in recognising that they are not a kind of determination that can be completely worked out, so as to make our experience into a systematic whole with reference to this particular form.

9. **Limitations of Perceptual Construction.** We are thus led on all hands to the general conclusion that perceptual construction, though valid enough within certain limits, is not an ultimately valid way of putting together an intelligible universe. It is valid in the sense that, when properly used, it can be made to work. A man or an animal is liable to deception in putting together objects by the help of sense-material; but either of them may learn by experience to put them together in a way that is coherent for all the purposes of action. For thought, however, such a collection of objects is unsatisfactory, because the methods by which it is put together are both

---

[1] See Hobhouse's *Theory of Knowledge*, Part I., chap. ii., §§ 5 and 6.

arbitrary in themselves and confined within arbitrary limits. Neither the material nor the way in which it is built up, nor the way in which it refuses to be built up, is intelligible. Hence the mind of a thinking being finds itself compelled to attempt other methods of construction.

CHAPTER II.

SCIENTIFIC CONSTRUCTION.

1. **The General Nature of Scientific Construction.** The construction by which knowledge is built up differs from perceptual construction by the presence of ideas and concepts and by the fact that it involves conscious activity. Common sense knowledge, however, as distinguished from that systematic knowledge which is called science, does little more than use consciously those modes of synthesis that are unconsciously used in perception. Hence it does not urgently demand any special consideration.[1] In scientific knowledge, on the other hand, there is an attempt at completeness and systematic order in particular directions; and this aim involves the use of more precise conceptions, or at least involves a more precise way of applying those conceptions that are used in a rough and ready manner in ordinary perception and in common sense knowledge. The chief of these conceptions are those quantitative (or

---

[1] From the psychological point of view, the study of the transition from perception to common sense knowledge is quite as interesting as the study of the transition from common sense to science; but, as it is essentially a stage of transition, I have thought it comparatively unimportant from the metaphysical point of view.

at least definitely ordered)[1] modes of determination that are rendered precise by the science of mathematics, and the two more concrete conceptions of Substance and Causation. These we must now briefly consider.

2. **Mathematical Conceptions.** All the most developed of the sciences tend to adopt mathematical methods of study; and, in proportion as they can adopt such methods, their statements become precise. This fact, however, is apt to convey a somewhat misleading impression with regard to the kind of knowledge that is contained in mathematics. The exactness of mathematical treatment is gained in general by limitation. It proceeds by hypothetical approximations to the truth; and these approximations sometimes involve a certain amount of distortion. In particular, mathematical treatment must in general involve an imperfect separation between the continuous and the discrete. Quantities have generally to be regarded as sums of units; and any quantity that is not of this nature can only be regarded as an ideal limit. On the other hand, the use of curves has sometimes the effect of tending to make discrete magnitudes appear as if they were continuous. Magnitudes that are strictly intensive do not appear to be capable of direct mathematical treatment at all. These limitations must always be borne in mind when the exactness and universality of mathematical truth are brought up for commendation.

Again, there is some danger of supposing that mathematical methods can be so employed as to outrun the limitations of the material to which they are applied. It is apt

---

[1] On the general conception of Order, reference may be made to the paper by Mr. Russell in *Mind*, New Series, Vol. x., p. 30.

to be thought, for instance, that we can be led by mathematical considerations to the apprehension of dimensions in space beyond the three that are set before us in actual experience. There seems to be no ground for thinking that mathematical constructions have any such claim to objective validity. A fourth dimension is a mere empty possibility unless it can be somehow verified in concrete experience. Similarly, in economics or in concrete physical science, the exactness of mathematical determinations must be held to apply only within the hypothetical limits that are assumed.[1]

3. **The Category of Substance.** The category of Substance connects itself with the element of identity in difference, which is present as an operative condition even in the purely perceptual consciousness, being implied in the ordinary perceptive recognition of objects.[2] Reflective thought, however, is led to seek to distinguish the element that remains the same from that which is variable. This attempt leads, as we have already to some extent noted, to the recognition of thinking and extended substances which remain essentially the same in the midst of their changing modes. But when we ask for a further definition of these substances, difficulties begin to present themselves. With regard to material substances, we are led to the conception of the persistence of Mass; and this may be interpreted as meaning the permanence of certain ultimate physical atoms. The attempt to make the nature of such atoms more precise, however, leads to the recognition that

---

[1] For a philosophical discussion of some of the most important modes of mathematical determination, reference may be made to Mr. Russell's book on *The Foundations of Geometry*.

[2] See Stout's *Manual of Psychology*, Book III., II., chap. i.

they cannot be regarded as in any ordinary sense physical at all ; they come to be thought of as vortex rings, rather than as solid bodies, and gradually we are led on to the conception of 'non-matter in motion,' in which the persistent element is stripped of its attributes, and becomes wholly incomprehensible.[1] All that seems to remain is a certain permanent possibility of particular modes of perceptual experience, coupled with a certain uniformity of transition which belongs rather to the conception of Causation than to that of Substance. On the whole, therefore, it seems at least doubtful whether the element that remains permanent can in the end be separated, even in thought, from that which changes in the case of material substance. With regard to the permanence of the Self, the same appears to be true. Here too we have permanent possibilities of certain modes of experience, together with certain uniformities of sequence in the experiences that actually arise, but nothing to which we can point as remaining absolutely constant in the midst of change. And thus the conception of Substance seems to do little more for us than lead us on to that of Causation.

4. **The Category of Causation.** Causation is generally recognised as the most fundamental of all the categories that are used in the scientific interpretation of the world. It is connected, like Substance, with the idea of uniformity in change, but relates primarily to a certain uniformity in the variant rather than in the constant. In the building up of experience it is probably first used in connection with the relation between conscious activity and changes in the objective world. Hence it is thought of as involving some

---

[1] See Ward's *Naturalism and Agnosticism*, Vol. I., p. 140.

active force and some passive thing that is operated upon. But the advance of scientific thought tends to remove this way of conceiving it, and to substitute the simple idea of a certain continuity and regularity in change. This abolishes in the end the distinction between cause and effect.[1] One thing is not thought of any longer as the cause of another ; but we are rather led to think simply of a certain continuity in events. Such continuity seems to furnish us with a good working conception in dealing with concrete events in experience, but is not capable of leading us to any complete systematisation of experience, or any absolute beginning in the series of events. There is no doubt also contained in the scientific conception of causation some idea of ground or explanation. Science, however, is quite unable to point to any ultimate grounds for the occurrence of events, except such as are contained in the idea of the persistence of certain qualities in that which changes—an idea which leads us back again to that of Substance. Beyond this, it has to content itself with the tracing of regular sequences.

5. **The Physical World.** By the help of the ideas of Substance and Cause in close conjunction, helped out by those of Number and Extensive Magnitude, we build up for ourselves the conception of the physical world as a system of things and events connected with one another in a continuous and uniform way. The development of the special physical sciences seems to show that the view of the world as thus constructed is capable of being worked out to an indefinite extent. But it seems doomed to incompleteness in its construction by the impossibility of reaching boundaries in Space, a real beginning or end in Time, an ultimate

---

[1] See Bradley's *Appearance and Reality*, Book I., chap. vi.

reality that endures, or a magnitude that is purely extensive and discrete.

6. **The World of Consciousness.** Over against this conception of the physical world, we build up the conception of the microcosm, the inner world of conscious process. Here also attempts have been made to apply the ideas of Substance and Causation, and to some extent—in spite of Kant's warning[1]—even mathematical determinations. But it is even more difficult in the case of conscious process than in that of physical change to point to anything that persists without alteration. In the sense, however, of the recognition of a certain continuity and uniformity of transition, it is possible to apply the ideas of Substance and Causation in a way very similar to that in which they are used in physical science; and the science of psychology results from the systematic effort to make use of them. The fact that psychical magnitudes are almost (if not quite) entirely continuous and intensive, makes the application of mathematical determinations more difficult—perhaps in the end impossible.[2]

7. **The Mechanical System of the Universe.** The possibility of forming for ourselves such a connected view of the physical world, on the one hand, and the world of conscious process on the other, has led to the conception of the possibility of a connected view of the whole universe of our experience as a complete system through which a stream

---

[1] *Metaphysical Rudiments of Physics*, Preface. Cf. Caird's *Critical Philosophy of Kant*, Vol. I., p. 617.

[2] Bradley's argument (see *Mind*, New Series, Vol. IV., pp. 1, 225) in favour of the applicability of extensive magnitude in Psychology is unconvincing, and indeed seems to contain some serious fallacies. But it is impossible to enter into the discussion of such a question in an outline like the present. Cf. Meinong's little book on Weber's Law.

of causal continuity can be traced. In a sense this is no doubt possible, and we shall have to return to the consideration of it at a later point. It may be possible, that is to say, to trace a definite and uniform relation between certain modes of physical organisation and the rise of consciousness, and to note, on the other hand, in a systematic way, the modes in which conscious process is connected with certain physical reactions. But the limitations of such causal continuity, as a means of scientific explanation, are made more apparent when such an extension is in contemplation. Space and movement in space are the chief facts that can be treated in a directly mathematical and mechanical fashion. The inadequacy of such modes of determination becomes apparent whenever we seek to apply them to qualitative or intensive differences, such as we find in life and thought. The impossibility of a complete mechanical system of the universe has been brought out in the recent work of Dr. James Ward,[1] and may perhaps be regarded as one of the few points that have been definitely established in metaphysical theory.

8. **Limitations of the World of Science.** Thus we are led to recognise, on the whole, that the world, as put together by scientific thought, though coherent as far as it goes, and capable of being made more and more coherent to a quite indefinite extent, is not capable of being made into a completely rounded and self-explanatory system by any commonly recognised method. The result of this conclusion may be to drive us into an attitude of simple philosophic doubt. But we are saved from this by the fact that the scientific view of the world is coherent, as far as it

---

[1] *Naturalism and Agnosticism*, Vol. I., lectures ii.-vi.

goes, and capable of indefinite extension. The attitude of the Agnostic is a more reasonable refuge—the view, that is to say, that we can attain to a coherent view of the universe from certain limited points of view, but that the nature of ultimate reality is unknown and unknowable. But before we accept this refuge, we have to consider some methods of synthesis, other than that of purely scientific construction, that may possibly be adopted. The chief of these would seem to be ethical construction, aesthetic construction, religious construction, and speculative construction. These we now proceed to examine in order.

CHAPTER III.

ETHICAL CONSTRUCTION.

1. The Moral Life as an Ideal Construction. When the constructions of physical science are felt to be unsatisfactory, either from lack of inner coherence or from the doubt that they throw on the ultimate value of the universe, men are often led to seek refuge in the constructions of the moral life. Of this tendency one of the most conspicuous instances is to be found in the case of Socrates. The discussions of the early Greek philosophers, especially when brought to a focus in the teaching of the Sophists, led on the whole to a general scepticism with regard to the possibility of a physical theory of the universe; and against this Socrates urged the possibility of a moral construction by reference to a clearly conceived chief end of man. It soon became apparent (especially through the discussions of Plato) that the latter necessitated a speculative construction as well; but Socrates, at least, does not appear to have had this in view. Similarly, in recent times, Carlyle, though with less scientific interest and more prophetic force, appealed to the moral consciousness against the consciousness of the physical world; but science was, perhaps, sufficiently revenged upon him by the ultimate incoherence of his ethical teaching. Further illustrations of the same antithesis in very various forms may be found in many periods of intellectual development. The Stoics and Epicureans, to a certain extent, represent it, though somewhat less definitely than Socrates. In more modern times, even Locke may be pointed to as one who maintained the possibility of an ethical theory which should be independent of our knowledge of the physical system. The importance of this became greater, as the sceptical results of his theory of knowledge became more apparent. Kant, Fichte, and even Comte may also be taken as representing, in different ways, something of the same tendency—something of the same general conviction that our moral constructions are less open to doubt than our physical constructions, or can yield an apprehension of some important truths that are inaccessible to purely scientific methods. In quite recent times we may also refer to Cardinal Newman,[1] Mr. Arthur Balfour,[2] and Professor W. James.[3] Even Professor Huxley represents, in his famous *Romanes Lecture*, the conviction that our moral constructions stand above the constructions of the physical system, and justify us in passing criticisms upon the latter.[4] In all these points of view, the ' Sollen ' (the ought) is in some way opposed to the ' Seyn ' (the simply existent), as something more directly issuing from the human mind itself, more thoroughly under the control

---

[1] *Grammar of Assent.*   [2] *Foundations of Belief.*

[3] *The Will to Believe.*

[4] Other writers who may be referred to, in the same general connection, are Professor W. Caldwell (*Schopenhauer's System in its Philosophical Significance,* and other writings) and Mr. H. Rutgers Marshall (*Instinct and Reason*). The main contention of Mr. B. Kidd's *Social Evolution* is closely connected with the same point of view.

of the will, and possessing, in some sense or other, a higher kind of validity.[1] It seems important, therefore, that we should inquire at this point into the precise metaphysical significance of such moral constructions. This we can hardly do without first attempting to give some general account of the nature of Will or Activity.

2. **The Meaning of Activity.** Activity is sometimes represented as a mysterious element in experience, an aspect of consciousness utterly different from feeling and knowledge, incapable of direct apprehension, and unintelligible except as a given fact.[2] In reality, however, activity seems to be little more than a name for consciousness itself, regarded in its own inner development. All consciousness is active, in the sense that it exists for itself, and has an independent movement of its own. The use of the term activity is, no doubt, like that of all terms that are applied to conscious process, in the first instance metaphorical.[3] When a horse pulls a cart, we say that the horse is active and the cart is passive, meaning that the initiation of movement is to be traced to the former and not to the latter.

---

[1] On this subject I may refer to an instructive paper by Professor Watson on " Recent Ethical Philosophy" in the *International Journal of Ethics* (Vol. IX., No. 4).

[2] The place assigned to Activity in Dr. Ward's *Naturalism and Agnosticism* is perhaps the least satisfactory aspect of that work. For discussions on the subject I may refer to Bradley's *Appearance and Reality*, Stout's *Analytic Psychology* (Book II., chap. i.), and the intermittent controversy between Bradley and Ward in *Mind*.

[3] There is no doubt another side to the question. *Part* of what we mean by activity is organic, rather than physical, and may be said to be transferred by metaphor to purely physical actions. This part seems to consist in sensations (of pressure, muscular movement, strain, etc.). But this part at least is clearly presentational.

But in consciousness we cannot point to any separable
things, like horse and cart, one of which may be said to act,
and the other to be acted upon. If we say that consciousness acts, we simply mean that some process takes place in
it which seems to find its explanation within consciousness
itself. Now it seems to be characteristic of all such process
that it points forwards, or is directed towards an end. This
end may be more or less explicitly conscious ; and the distinction commonly drawn between activity and passivity
seems to turn on the degree in which an end is consciously
before us. When the movement of consciousness is
explicitly guided by the thought of an end, we say
that the mind is in an active state ; whereas in the
seemingly aimless movement of a dream or reverie we
say that it is comparatively passive. If there is any
mystery in activity—apart from the relation between
conscious process and bodily process—it must lie in
this possibility of looking forward, or of being guided by
a conscious end.

3. **The End of Action.** The metaphysical importance
of this fact of activity lies chiefly in its introduction of
the idea of finality, as opposed to the simple sequence
of changes which alone we seem able to discover in the
physical world. Hence it is not surprising that the first
definite introduction of the idea of final cause in ancient
Greek speculation took place in connection with the
doctrine of Anaxagoras, that mind is the explanation of
the ordered system of the universe.[1] It seemed to both
Plato and Aristotle that this doctrine involved the recogni-

---

[1] Anaxagoras himself does not seem to have had any real apprehension of the idea of finality. See Burnet's *Early Greek Philosophy*, p. 292.

tion of purpose in the structure of the world.[1] Modern psychology is on the whole equally explicit in urging that we cannot see the real significance of psychical process without taking account of the aim that is, consciously or unconsciously, involved in it.[2] To say this is of course not to maintain that conscious processes necessarily point to something beyond themselves. On the contrary, it would seem that, the more clearly the aim in psychical process is discovered, the more fully does it appear to be of the nature of self-realisation, or at least of self-unfolding. Activity seems in the end to mean, as Aristotle perceived,[3] the actualisation of what is from the first implicit.

4. **Conduct.** This process of actualisation, however, involves relations with things and persons distinct from the conscious process to which they are related ; and the working out of the individual life in relation to such things and persons is what we understand by Conduct. In conduct the end aimed at may be more or less unconscious —i.e. it may not be clearly defined before consciousness ; but there is always some object of pursuit sufficiently definite to be chosen as a good and to suggest means for its attainment.

5. **The Good.** We are thus led to the idea of a Good. Aristotle said that the Good might be defined as that at which all things aim.[4] Perhaps it would be more satisfactory to say that it is that which is involved as an end in any case of aiming at an object. It seems possible to aim at things which are not really regarded as good

---

[1] See Plato's *Phaedo*, 97-9, and Aristotle's *Metaphysics*, Book I.
[2] See Stout's *Analytic Psychology*, Vol. I., p. 189.
[3] See Zeller's *Aristotle*, chap. vii.
[4] *Nicomachean Ethics*, Book I., chap. i.

either by the person who aims at them or by impartial
spectators looking on. But in such cases there is an
indirect aim at something else; and it is this implicit
end that ought to be regarded as the good.

6. **The Nature of Ultimate Good**. The idea of Good
being thus involved in the nature of consciousness, it
is not surprising that many should have been led to regard
it as something purely subjective. If happiness is 'our
being's end and aim,' and is immanent in the very nature
of that being, it seems but a step farther to say that it
is nothing but a state of consciousness, and is essentially
independent of any objective reference. 'The mind is its
own place,' says Milton's Satan, 'and in itself can make
a Heaven of Hell, a Hell of Heaven.'[1] The ancient
Cynics and Stoics brought out this subjective aspect of
human happiness. The 'Wise Man' of the Stoics was
supposed to realise the highest good, under whatever
conditions his life might be passed. But it is in the
doctrine of Hedonism that this point of view is carried
farthest. From this point of view the good for man is
that which is most purely subjective, viz.: the feeling of
pleasure. Some of the early Hedonists held that this
feeling can be made quite independent of external conditions; so that it was possible to exclaim, even in the

---

[1] Contrast this with the well-known lines of Browning :

> " One place performs, like any other place,
> The proper service every place on earth
> Was framed to furnish man with."
>
> *Red Cotton Nightcap Country.*

Here the primacy of the subjective side is emphasised, while at the
same time the function of the objective side is duly acknowledged.

torture of the rack, 'how sweet!'[1]   Most Hedonists, however, have considered pleasure and pain as dependent on
objective conditions; but they have maintained that the
value of those objective conditions as elements in the
Good for man depends entirely on the pleasure or pain
that arises from them.

The most carefully reasoned form of this doctrine is
probably that presented by the late Dr. Henry Sidgwick.[2]
His contention is, in the first place, that nothing external
to consciousness can be regarded as the Good for man.
It must be some mode of desirable consciousness.   Then
he urges, further, that even among modes of consciousness
those that involve an objective content are not in the
end valued for their own sakes, but only for their purely
subjective accompaniments or products.   Pleasure is thus
in the end the only thing that is valued for itself, the only
ultimate good.

Such reasoning, however, seems to be fallacious.   The
fact that no object apart from consciousness can be regarded
as a good does not show that states of consciousness could
be a good without reference to objects.   Similarly, the fact
that states of consciousness containing an objective reference
are not valued for their own sakes without reference to their
subjective accompaniments or products does not show that
these accompaniments or products would be valued by us
without reference to the objective content on which they
depend.   The truth seems to be rather that human experience cannot in reality be split up in the way that is here
supposed.   A pure feeling without objective reference could

[1] See Zeller's *Stoics, Epicureans, and Sceptics*, p. 477.
[2] *Methods of Ethics*, Book III., chap. xiv.

not be regarded as a good by a human consciousness. All human pleasure is pleasure in something. It is true that if that something gave no pleasure, we should not be able to value it; but still, seeing that it does please us, we do value *it*, and not simply the pleasure that it yields.

7. **The Good as Self-realisation.** The necessity of thinking of the Good for man as involving an objective content, as well as a subjective feeling, led Aristotle to think of it as a kind of self-realisation; and a similar conception has been used by some of the most prominent ethical writers in recent times. This way of conceiving the good serves to bring out both the subjective and the objective aspect of it. The fact that it is thought of as *self*-realisation brings out its significance as the unfolding of the end involved from the first in the nature of conscious process; while, on the other hand, the fact that it is thought of as self-*realisation* (not self-satisfaction) serves to remind us that the unfolding of the end is not a mere standing still within conscious process. Even this expression, however, still tends to throw the emphasis somewhat unduly on the subjective side of the good. If we continue to use it, we must remember that it means, not merely the unfolding of the self, but the filling of the self with reality.[1] It means such an unfolding of the conscious nature of the individual as shall enable him fully to grasp the content of his world and adjust it harmoniously in relation to himself. Thus conceived, self-realisation cannot be purely inward or subjective. The consideration

---

[1] See Mr. A. E. Taylor's article in the *International Journal of Ethics* —" Self realisation—a Criticism," Vol. VI., No. 3. Reference may also be made to the same writer's recent work on *The Problem of Conduct*. For further discussion of the nature of Good, see Bradley's *Appearance and Reality*, Book II., chap. xxv.

of its meaning leads directly to a study of the relation of the individual to his world.

8. The Social System. When we study the relation of the individual to his world, what first becomes apparent is the importance of the relationships of persons to one another as contributing to the realisation of a common good. The good for man, if in the end it may be called an individual good, is at any rate not realisable through a purely individual effort. The individual comes to himself, if we may so express it, through the discipline of social relations. It is here that the view of human life taken by Plato and Aristotle is so markedly superior to that of the Cynics, and even to that of the later Stoics and to many modern theories. It seems impossible to conceive the development of an intelligent life in the midst of an unintelligible world, or even in the midst of a world which is otherwise unintelligent. If the macrocosm were a chaos, the microcosm could contain nothing but madness. The mind grows by organising for itself a system of intelligible objects; and can only realise itself as an intelligence by finding its unity reflected in the world around it. This it finds most completely in the life of other intelligent beings that develop along with it; and we have no real means of understanding how a mind could grow apart from such a social medium.[1]

9. The Moral Universe. We are thus led to think of the individual as realising his good in common with others. This common good may be thought of at first,

---

[1] Cf. Caird's *Critical Philosophy of Kant*, Book II., chaps. vi. and vii. ; and Bosanquet's *Philosophical Theory of the State*, especially chap. xi.

after the manner of Comte, as the realisation of a purely human perfection in the midst of an alien physical or phenomenal world. The social order, or the general system of Humanity, may be opposed to the system of the world at large. Such an opposition would seem to be implied in the view of Huxley set forth in his celebrated *Romanes Lecture*, to which reference has already been made. The cosmic system, from this point of view, comes to be thought of as a mechanical struggle, without definite end; while the life of man is regarded as containing within it ideal aspirations that carry him above the tendencies of the cosmic system. But further reflection seems to show that the good for man could not really be attained in a hostile universe. Human life can after all only be understood as part of the natural order, though it may contain explicit ends that are not apparent in the ordinary processes of nature. To suppose that there is a radical opposition between the human and the cosmic systems would be to land ourselves hopelessly in the old dilemma, whether it is better to be a fool or a knave. To set ourselves in opposition to the inherent tendencies of the natural world could hardly be other than folly. Such a dilemma does no doubt often seem to present itself in the modern conception of life. When, for instance, it is urged that it is only through the struggle for existence that the highest type of life can be realised, and yet that moral progress means the continual weakening of the struggle, we are at once led to ask—Are we to help moral progress, or are we to help human progress? Attempts are sometimes made to evade this difficulty by saying that in the individual life the moral aim should prevail, but that there must be a constant struggle in international affairs. But if the natural struggle for existence is the road to progress, it seems clear that the individual as well as the nation must be bound to pursue it. How can moral progress mean something different from human progress? If we oppose the cosmic process to the moral process, the latter must in the end inevitably be sacrificed.

10. **Limitations of Ethical Construction.** Such considerations may perhaps suffice to bring home to us that ethical construction, as opposed to other modes of the synthesis of our experience, cannot be accepted as final. It is not final, because it cannot be regarded as complete in itself. Moral realisation is only possible in a universe that is intrinsically adapted to the realisation of a moral good. It may even be said that there is an inner contradiction in the demand of the moral life. It urges us to realise a good that is not yet real; and yet can only make this demand intelligible by postulating that the universe is after all in harmony with the good that is sought. We begin with an opposition between what ought to be and what is, and yet end by postulating that what is must be supposed to be in harmony with what ought to be. This contradiction might no doubt be overcome, by saying that the moral 'ought' is only opposed to a limited mode of reality, or to reality as viewed from a limited standpoint; and that what it brings out is something that lies deeper in the nature of things, or that corresponds to a more complete view of what reality is or involves. But to say this implies a faith that carries us beyond the point of view of simple morality, and that seems to require further justification.

Such a justification may be sought by passing from the point of view of morality to that of art or religion. The constructions contained in them are what we must next consider.

CHAPTER IV.

AESTHETIC CONSTRUCTION.

1. **The Beautiful as Ideal Construction.** The failure of the ethical construction seemed to be due in part to the impossibility of treating it as subjective. It carried us out inevitably to the consideration of an objective system of the universe. In the search for a more purely subjective mode of construction, we are naturally led to Aesthetics; and it is in art that many of the finest natures have sought a refuge from the apparent brutality of objective fact. "Art still has truth—take refuge there." The judgment of taste may no doubt seem at first to have an even more definitely objective foundation than that which is pronounced on conduct. Things are beautiful or ugly, it may be said, just as they are large or small, green or red; whereas the rightness or wrongness of actions depends more obviously on some standard that we bring to bear upon them. The moral life might seem, from this point of view, to be more purely our own than the world of beauty. On reflection, however, one is very soon led to an opposite conclusion; and the subjectivity of taste, about which there is proverbially no disputing, begins to be emphasised. The objectivity of the judgment is then

seen to mean little more than its directness or immediacy, due to the fact that it depends on simple feeling. But if feeling is the most direct form of consciousness, it is also the most purely subjective. Here then, it may be thought, we find something at last that is satisfying as a mode of construction, and yet independent of any objective system of the universe. It does not, like the activity involved in conduct, point to an end that has to be realised, and that implies objective conditions. It rather seems to contain the realisation immediately within itself. "Beauty is its own excuse for being," the poets tell us; and again, "Love is victory, the prize itself." The artist no doubt may be regarded as a moral worker. He at least has an end in view: he seeks a good which must, it would seem, be regarded as part of the general good for man. But Aesthetics is not primarily concerned with art,[1] but rather with the conditions involved in the apprehension of the beautiful; and this, though containing a mental construction, presents itself rather as a direct intuition than as the pursuit of an end. The consideration of this mode of construction thus leads us to reflect on the nature of feeling, just as the consideration of the last led us to reflect on the nature of activity.

2. **The Nature of Feeling.** Feeling, like activity, is sometimes represented as a mysterious and unaccountable element in consciousness. It is spoken of as if it were a kind of Kantian 'thing *per se*.' It has the two sides of

---

[1] I am inclined to think that students of Aesthetics have in general erred by confining their attention too exclusively to artistic creation, instead of to the more general question of the apprehension of the beautiful. But this is an *obiter dictum*, which I cannot here attempt to justify. On the other side, see Bosanquet's *Aesthetic*, p. 3.

pleasure and pain, but otherwise is simple, unanalysable,
unpresentable. But there seems to be some error in this.
It can hardly be unpresentable if we can distinguish degrees
in it, or even the two qualities of agreeable and disagreeable.[1] Yet it appears to be right to distinguish feeling
from the ordinary presentational material of consciousness.
It seems to depend on the relation of this material to
the unity within which it is presented, and to be a kind
of direct sense of value or worth, in relation to the end
that is implicit in all conscious process. Further, it seems
to admit of differences of kind or quality, according to the
nature of the unity within which it arises, or of the end
that is implicitly present. At the lowest level of pure
sensation it is perhaps correctly described as a simple
tone of the sensation that it accompanies.[2] At higher
levels it appears to become more complex and more
definitely of the nature of an appreciation of value or
worth. Aesthetic appreciation is one of its highest and
most intellectual forms.

3. **Feeling as Constructive Power**. Feeling, as is very
generally recognised, is very closely related to action.
This is sometimes expressed by saying that feeling is
the cause of action. If cause means simply unconditional
antecedent, there is some justification for this, at least
on the understanding that sequence does not necessarily
imply an interval of time. If it means 'ground,' the statement is more open to doubt. Perhaps it is best to say
that changes in conscious process, so far as they are
subjectively conditioned, proceed in accordance with

---

[1] See above, Book II., chap. ii., § 6.
[2] See Stout's *Manual of Psychology*, Book II., chap. viii.

the character of the accompanying feeling.[1]   In the case
of the appreciation of the beautiful, the accompanying form
of activity is seen in the impulse to artistic creation, and
also in the more purely contemplative impulse to discover
the beautiful in nature.   Such impulses differ from the
activities involved in moral action, inasmuch as they do
not contain the express recognition of any ultimate end.

4. **Beauty and Pleasure.**   What has so far been stated
evidently implies that the beautiful is to be regarded as
a form of the pleasant.   That this is broadly true seems
clear ; but it is important to note the exact kind of pleasure
that is involved.   We have recognised distinctions of
kind among pleasures.   The lover of the beautiful, the
poet or artist, is not simply to be classed among pleasure-
seekers.   Yet in a sense he is a pleasure-seeker,

> " Content if he may but enjoy
>   The things which others understand."

What he seeks is an intellectual pleasure, the joy of
insight.   Beauty is, as Bradley puts it,[2] the ' self-existent
pleasant,' the pleasant as an intellectual object.   It must
be observed, however, that the recognition of this at once
involves a modification of the view according to which
the appreciation of the beautiful is something purely
subjective.   If the beautiful is the pleasant for thought, it is
essentially the objectively pleasant.   The feeling involved,
though in itself subjective, has a direct reference to reality.

---

[1] The exact relation between feeling and activity has perhaps not yet
been precisely determined.   The discussions by Ehrenfels (*Ueber Fühlen
und Wollen*) are instructive.   Cf. *Mind*, New Series, Vol. IV., pp.
427-9, and Stout's *Analytic Psychology*, Book I., chap. vi., and Book
II., chap. xii., § 9.

[2] *Appearance and Reality*, p. 464.

5. **The Beautiful and the Good.** This brings us back to the question whether, after all, the beautiful can be distinguished from the good. Both would seem to have a subjective reference, while yet at the same time both imply an objective content. The main differences would seem to be (1) that the Good is an end to be aimed at, while the beautiful is something apprehended as realised, (2) that the attainment of the good involves a process of adaptation of means to end, while the beautiful is apprehended by direct intuition. But it may be urged that if both mean what ultimately satisfies the aspirations of a thinking being, they cannot really be distinct. Hence Goethe says that the beautiful is higher than the good, including the good within it. It would seem to be the higher and more comprehensive of the two, as involving the attainment of that which is only aimed at in the other. The good, it may be said, so far as it is attained, is beautiful; it differs from the beautiful only as involving struggle. This, however, would be a somewhat one-sided way of looking at the matter. It may be true to say that the final significance of the beautiful and the good, as that which in the end gives satisfaction to a reasonable being, is identical; and that in this identity it is the striving involved in the pursuit of the good that disappears, leaving only the beautiful. In this sense it may be maintained that the beautiful is more ultimate, and more free from contradiction than the good. But the beautiful also is a process; it has its degrees and grades, and it is only its ultimate form, its final perfection, that could be said to include the good in itself. The good may be said, on the other hand, to be higher than the beautiful, inasmuch as it involves, even in its lower phases, the

strenuous pursuit of the ultimate end ; whereas, in the case
of the beautiful, we are satisfied at each stage with the
end that is there and then realised, however incomplete
it may be.   Taking the beautiful, however, in the sense
of the highest type of beauty, we may no doubt say that
this is identical with the highest good, and involves the
supersession of the struggle involved in the pursuit of the
good, and the solution of the contradictions that this
pursuit appears to contain.[1]

6. **Beauty and Truth.**   When the beautiful is thus
conceived in relation to the good, its relation to truth
is also made apparent.   The good, as we have seen, has
to be thought of in the end as the realisation of the deepest
meaning of things.   Beauty also, in the sense in which
it includes the good, must be supposed to imply the apprehension of this deepest meaning of reality.   This is no
doubt what Keats had in mind in saying that " Beauty
is truth, truth beauty."   What is implied is that things
are not really grasped in their truth unless they are seen
in that harmonious relation to the whole which yields
complete aesthetic satisfaction.   It seems clear, however,
that the recognition of this involves a faith no less profound
in the ultimate harmony of the system of the universe
than that which is contained in the moral consciousness.
From this point of view the subjectivity of the beautiful
can no longer be maintained.

7. **The Objectivity of the Beautiful.**   The attempt to
represent the appreciation of the beautiful as purely sub-

---

[1] For further discussion of the general nature of the beautiful,
reference may be made to Bradley's *Appearance and Reality*, pp.
463-466, and Bosanquet's *History of Aesthetic*, pp. 4-5.

jective seems to rest on the same sort of illusion as that which gives rise to Hedonism in Ethics. It is first seen that aesthetic appreciation is a form of feeling. Then it is urged that feeling is essentially subjective, and hence that the objective side in aesthetic appreciation can have no importance. In this it is not recognised that, though aesthetic appreciation is feeling, it is intellectual feeling; and intellectual feeling means the appreciation of something as having objective significance. No doubt there are degrees in which this intellectual element is present in aesthetic appreciation. At its lowest level it amounts to little more than ordinary feeling of pleasure. The appreciation of beautiful colour may be little more than a sensational feeling-tone. The lover of the beautiful at such a level as this is not much superior to the ordinary pleasure-seeker. But at its higher levels aesthetic appreciation is a form of intellectual insight. So regarded, however, it raises the question how far the insight contained in it is reliable.

8. **Aesthetic Values.** We may connect what has just been urged with the view that feeling involves an appreciation of value or worth. This also may be regarded as purely subjective or as containing an objective element. In reality it would seem that there is always at least an implicitly objective aspect of feeling. Even the lowest form of feeling, as simple tone of sensation, involves in reality the appreciation of something as heightening the general vitality or the activity of some particular organ. This is no doubt only implicit in simple feeling; but in the higher forms of feeling this objective reference becomes more and more explicit. In aesthetic feeling, in particular, there is involved the recognition of a kind of value or

worth in the world that we apprehend. Such worth may at first simply be taken to mean that we value it; but we soon go on to affirm that it really is *valuable*,[1] *i.e.* deserving of being valued by every consciousness that apprehends it. This view of the world as a system of objective values is the faith that is implicit in aesthetic appreciation.

9. **Limitations of Aesthetic Construction**. It would appear from all this, that aesthetic construction contains a limitation somewhat similar to that involved in ethical construction. It does not, indeed, involve the inner contradiction that the latter displays in the opposition of what ought to be to what is. What we apprehend as beautiful *is* beautiful; it is not merely something that we seek to make beautiful. The limitation appears simply in the opposition of the subjective to the objective. If the question is raised—How do we know that this is beautiful? we may attempt to answer it in two different ways. One is to say, I feel that it is beautiful; but this rests it on the purely subjective side. Another way is to say, I know that it is beautiful, because I see it as having value in relation to the harmonious system of the universe. This is the objective answer; but this implies a theory of the universe, which carries us beyond the simple appreciation of the beautiful. In short, the appreciation of the beautiful is in this dilemma; it cannot rest in itself, but must either become simple pleasure-seeking or a theory of the universe. When it becomes a theory of the universe, it seems to be indistinguishable from religion.

---

[1] On the connection between value and valuing, reference should be made to the discussions by Meinong and Ehrenfels. Cf. *Mind*, New Series, Vol. IV., pp. 434-5.

CHAPTER V.

RELIGIOUS CONSTRUCTION.

1. **Religion as Ideal Construction.** Religion may perhaps be best regarded as the explicit recognition of the faith that is ultimately involved in ethical and aesthetic construction.[1] No doubt it may be said that not everything commonly classed as a religion does embody any such faith. Some so-called religions are only superstitious adorations of supposed superior powers. It is generally recognised, however, that forms of worship that rest simply on fear are not properly to be called religion. Religion must involve some form of reverence. Worship is properly, as Carlyle was fond of urging,[2] the recognition of something as having *worth*, and indeed as having the highest worth. Religion is thus very closely connected with that apprehension of ultimate value which is implied in

---

[1] The English reader will probably find the best general account of the nature and growth of religion in Dr. Edward Caird's *Evolution of Religion* and the late Principal Caird's *Fundamental Ideas of Christianity*. The discussions in Bradley's *Appearance and Reality* will also be found very instructive. See Book II., chap. xxv.

[2] *Past and Present, Latter Day Pamphlets, On Heroes*, etc.

aesthetic appreciation, and through that with the ethical apprehension of an ultimate good or end of human action.

2. **General Nature of Religion.** Religion, thus understood, implies a theory of the universe. As distinguished from a philosophical system, however, it has the characteristic of intuitive apprehension. It may, indeed, be buttressed up by evidences and proofs; but these are generally felt to be a weakness rather than a strength, from the point of view of religious faith. The strongest faith on the whole rests on the evidence of the heart.[1] Hence it is sometimes said that religion is essentially an affair of feeling; and thus we are brought back once more to the opposition between the subjective and the objective. It may be said at once, however, that religion at any rate aims at being more than subjective. There is such a thing as a dilettante aestheticism, which aims at nothing further than a purely subjective enjoyment, and is wholly indifferent to the truth or falsehood of

---

[1] This aspect of the religious consciousness is well expressed in Tennyson's *In Memoriam*, cxxiv. :

> " I found Him not in world or sun,
>   Or eagle's wing, or insect's eye;
> Nor through the questions men may try,
>   The petty cobwebs we have spun :
>
> If e'er when faith had fall'n asleep,
>   I heard a voice 'believe no more,'
> And heard an ever-breaking shore
>   That tumbled in the Godless deep ;
>
> A warmth within the breast would melt
>   The freezing reason's colder part,
> And like a man in wrath the heart
>   Stood up and answer'd 'I have felt.'"

that in which it takes delight; and it is possible to take an interest of this kind in religious ceremonials and even in religious feelings. But no one would call a man who took such a dilettante interest in matters connected with religion a religious man. No one can be religious in any true sense of the word without a firm conviction of the objective truth of the main points in his faith. It is this firm belief in the objective reality of its subject-matter that gives religion its earnestness. An artist with a similar conviction of the objective worth of the beautiful would be essentially a religious artist. Goethe and Keats might perhaps among poets be fairly so described. This earnestness of conviction brings religion into the closest relationship to conduct. What is thus firmly believed must influence action, and must even presuppose action.[1] It seems erroneous, however, to define religion, as Matthew Arnold did, as morality touched with emotion.[2] This omits the conviction of reality which is the very essence of religion. It might be nearer the truth to say that religion is the firm and intuitive conviction that reality is right. Its simplest expression is that which is given to it by Browning :

> " God's in His Heaven,
> All's right with the world."

---

[1] On the relation between Belief and Action, see Stout's *Manual of Psychology*, Book IV., chap. viii., § 2, which, however, probably contains some exaggeration on this point.

[2] We, in this country, are perhaps apt to connect religion too exclusively with morality. The British, like the Jews, are a pre-eminently active people, and tend to look for what is highest in life in the realization of their practical energies. More sensuous, more emotional, and more contemplative peoples do not as a rule connect religion so directly with the active moral life.

3. **The World as One, Beautiful and Good.** More definitely we may say that the faith involved in all real religion seems to amount to the conviction that the world is one, beautiful and good, thus combining the results of the scientific, aesthetic, and ethical constructions.

It is difficult for the religious consciousness to avoid the conviction that the world is one, or at least that the power that is deepest and most fundamental in it is one; otherwise there is no firm basis for the conviction that it makes for what is best. If there is more than one power, there will be a conflict of ends. Hence it is at least partly true to represent what has been called ' cosmic emotion,' the feeling connected with the thought of the unity of the world, as specially characteristic of the religious consciousness.[1]

The religious consciousness also thinks of the world as beautiful; for it is represented as a completely harmonious system, satisfying the deepest demands of the intellectual nature. This at least seems to be what all the higher forms of religion aim at.

This harmonious unity is, moreover, conceived as that in which is realised all that is highest in the good man's aims, and that which contains the ultimate ground and justification of these aims.

Thus the world, as conceived by the religious consciousness, is one, beautiful, and good.

4. **Types of Religion.** It is evident that among the great religions of the world the elements to which reference has now been made are contained in very varying

---

[1] See Clifford's *Lectures and Essays.*

degrees.[1] In general the religions that most emphasise the element of unity are those that approximate to the pantheistic type; the element of beauty is perhaps best represented by the polytheistic type; while monotheism contains most distinctly the recognition of the good, though generally thought of in contrast to a principle of evil, against which it struggles. It is doubtful, however, whether any real religion that has had a firm hold on mankind has been wholly destitute of any of them. The Jewish religion was mainly ethical, but the idea of the unity of the world is also strongly marked in the background. The idea of beauty is much less prominent, as it is also in Christianity, but is not wholly absent. Medieval art endeavoured to make good the deficiencies of Christianity in this respect. The religion of the Greeks, on the other hand, was strongest on this side, but with the other elements also continually tending to rise into prominence. The so-called Religion of Humanity is an attempt to make religion purely ethical. By so doing, however, even the ethical faith, that the world is essentially good, is lost.[2] Probably just for this reason there seems no real prospect that that form of religion will ever prevail. The more purely intellectual type of religion is best seen in writers like Plato, Aristotle, and Spinoza.

5. **The Problem of Evil.** The most difficult problem

---

[1] Religion is one of those concrete concepts that cannot be satisfactorily defined by the method of singling out a common element in all its particular forms. See above, Book II., chap. iv., § 3. What we have to attempt is rather to find out the type to which its highest modes of development tend to approximate. Cf. Caird's *Evolution of Religion*, Vol. I., Lecture Second.

[2] Buddhism is perhaps a better type of the purely ethical religion.

with which the religious consciousness—at least in its more speculative forms—is confronted, is that of finding a place for evil in a world that has to be conceived as essentially one, beautiful, and good. The existence of evil, both physical and moral, is too apparent to be altogether set aside; and indeed the religious spirit, through its vivid insistence on moral principle, tends rather to emphasise the sense of sin and imperfection in the world as it actually appears. Yet, if the world is to be regarded as ultimately good, it would seem that evil must in the end be treated as unreal. The Manichean view, according to which there is a real independent principle of evil in the world, seems incompatible in the end with the religious attitude. If the Devil is to be recognised as real, it cannot be as an independent principle, but at most as the necessary counterpart of God. In the more speculative forms of religion evil tends to be represented as existing only as a means for the realisation of good. Perhaps the most striking expression of this point of view in recent times is that contained in the poetry of Robert Browning.[1] According to this view, goodness, joy, perfection of life, can only be achieved through conflict with evil, pain, and defect. A difficulty is, however, always felt in working out this position. While it is easy to show that much of what is best in life is realised through the conflict with evil, it is difficult to convince men that good cannot exist at all except as the negation of evil.[2] Plato held[3] that, while some pleasure

---

[1] See the very interesting books by Professor Henry Jones, *Browning as a Philosophical and Religious Teacher*, and Mr. A. C. Pigou, *Robert Browning as a Religious Teacher*.

[2] See on this point Mr. Pigou's book, pp. 87, 91, etc.

[3] *Republic*, Book IX.

is only the negation of pain, real pleasure has a positive and independent existence; and it is apt to be felt, in like manner, that all real good ought to be positive and independent. But the consideration of such problems leads us over to the speculative point of view.

6. **The Validity of Religion.** The fact that religion claims to be a kind of intuitive insight makes it peculiarly difficult to establish it on grounds. It is a thing of which men are persuaded, not something that can be proved to them. The grounds that they seek are not logical grounds, but grounds that awaken belief, grounds that satisfy the feelings and the will rather than the pure intellect. When men begin to search for logical grounds of belief, there is an implication of doubt, which is almost fatal to the religious attitude of mind. Hence we generally find that religions are supported by ceremonies, by mythologies that appeal to the imagination, by sanctions, by anything rather than by logical proof. When, however, distrust arises with regard to the ground on which religion rests, there is nothing for it but to fall back on metaphysics. Proofs of the being of God then begin to take the place of mystic rites, marvellous traditions, and terrible threats. But though metaphysics may supply a substitute for religion, it is doubtful whether it can properly be said to restore it. Plato and Spinoza may be called religious philosophers; but such philosophic religion is very different from what is commonly understood by the term. The philosophical attitude of mind may have many elements akin to those of religion, as it may have much that is akin to poetry; but it cannot properly be either poetic or religious. Its attitude of questioning is incompatible with the directness of both. But perhaps it would be truer to say that they

all find what they ultimately aim at in an attitude of mind which is above all of them as they exist apart.[1]

7. Limitations of Religious Construction. From what has now been said the limitations of the religious mode of construction must be sufficiently apparent. It rests on feeling, and yet emphatically insists on the objectivity of its content. It is an intuitive apprehension, yet the completeness of that which it professes to discover requires an absolute proof which could only be mediately given. It is a sort of half-way house between the direct acceptance of the world as presented to us by the senses and speculative construction. It tries to make the results of speculative insight palpable to the imagination. It shows the universe as a picture, the aim of life as a threat, duty as a blow, the final good as a caress. Such figurative presentation is soon seen to be inadequate to the nature of the objects that we are trying to set before ourselves.[2] Hence the need for a more speculative mode of construction.

---

[1] Some interesting remarks on this point will be found in M'Taggart's *Studies in the Hegelian Dialectic*, pp. 229-230.

[2] Cf. Wallace's *Prolegomena to Hegel's Logic*, chap. xxiii.

CHAPTER VI.

SPECULATIVE CONSTRUCTION.

1. **General Nature of Speculative Construction.** It is the aim of speculative construction to carry on the work of the particular sciences, so as to reach a view of the system of experience as a whole. From this point of view, speculative construction connects itself in the closest way with scientific construction. In thus carrying on the work of the sciences, however, the speculative thinker is in general not merely influenced by a scientific motive, but is stimulated also by the hope that, through this systematic construction, satisfaction will be found for the ethical, aesthetic, and religious demands of a thinking being. This hope seems to be justified by the fact that the purely scientific demands could hardly be satisfied without carrying the satisfaction of the others along with them. If, indeed, the mechanical system of the universe could be accepted as the last word about it, there would be no satisfaction in this for those other needs of our nature. Nor is it enough to say, with Spencer,[1] that satisfaction can be found for the most fundamental of them by the

---

[1] *First Principles*, Part I., chap. v.

mere denial that the mechanical system can be worked out. But if the world could be seen as a real unity for thought, this unity must from the nature of the case have that complete harmony with the needs of thought which is required to give satisfaction to the demands of religion —which, as we have seen, may be regarded as including the ethical and aesthetic demands. In this sense, therefore, we may accept the general view of Spencer, that it is the great aim of speculative thought to conciliate the demands of science and religion.

2. **Ultimate Reality.** This speculative ideal of a completely coherent system of experience is commonly described as the Absolute. The Absolute is sometimes thought of in such a way as to make it seem impossible that it should be known. This is of course most definitely done by such writers as Mr. Herbert Spencer and others who call themselves Agnostics. In a somewhat less complete way it is set beyond the reach of positive knowledge by such philosophers as Kant, and is represented as only an object of faith or belief. The arguments against the possibility of knowing the Absolute have also been put with much force by Sir W. Hamilton,[1] though his general point of view is not quite that understood by the term Agnosticism. But all such contentions may be criticised as implying either a mistaken view of the nature of knowledge or a false conception of what is meant by the Absolute. The Absolute is apt to be thought of as that which is free from all relations; and it is then easy enough to show that what is destitute of all relations can

---

[1] *Discussions.* Cf. also Mill's *Examination of Sir William Hamilton's Philosophy*, chaps. iv. and v.

supply nothing of which thought could possibly take hold. This is particularly easy when the work of thought is definitely conceived as that of establishing relations between things previously given. But the general view of knowledge that we have already set forth may suffice to convince us that this is a serious misconception of its nature. Still, even when such criticisms are allowed their full force, it remains true in a certain sense that the Absolute must lie beyond the range of human knowledge. It is of the essence of the conception of the Absolute that it should involve perfect completeness; whereas it seems clear that human knowledge sets out from the part and can never hope to reach the whole. This does not, however, interfere with the possibility of the attainment of a general conception of what is involved in the nature of the Absolute, or even with the attainment of some kind of intellectual conviction of its reality. It does perhaps prevent anything of the nature of complete certainty. The ontological argument, which alone seems capable of establishing the reality of the Absolute, does not appear to carry complete conviction.[1]

3. **Types of Speculative Construction.** The attempts that have been made at a real speculative construction, in the sense that has now been indicated, are comparatively few, and have in general a strong family likeness. Of

---

[1] The essence of the ontological argument would seem to be that what can be completely thought out must be real; and the fatal flaw in it lies in the fact that the thought of the Absolute never is completely thought out. Mr. Bradley's statement of the ontological argument in *Appearance and Reality* (chap. xxiv.) is probably one of the best. Among earlier attempts are those of Anselm, Descartes, Leibniz, and Hegel. See Windelband's *History of Philosophy.*

course in the history of philosophy, as commonly set
forth, many views are included which would not meet our
present requirements at all.   Sceptical and agnostical
positions are commonly dealt with in the history of philosophy as fully as those of a constructive character, and
are sometimes even spoken of as philosophical systems—as
if, as Hegel expressed it,[1] darkness were a kind of light.
Nor again would systems of a mystical kind be speculative
constructions in the sense here understood.   Anything that
rests on intuition, rather than on reasoned insight, would
be more akin to religion, as that has been here conceived,
than to a properly speculative system.   On this ground,
such systems as those of Plotinus, Böhme, and perhaps
even Schelling, might for our present purpose be set aside.

Even some systems that may be more definitely described as involving a real intellectual construction are
practically excluded from consideration at this point by
our previous discussions.   A dualism, for instance, like
that of Descartes could hardly be regarded as a solution
of the speculative problem, as here conceived.   As a
matter of fact, it broke down hopelessly in the hands of
his followers, and would now be generally recognised as
utterly inadequate for the purpose.   A materialism again,
like that of Hobbes, is simply an attempt to work out
what has been here described as a purely scientific construction; and the unsatisfactoriness of this has already
been sufficiently seen.   Nor would a subjective construction, like that of Berkeley,[2] meet our present requirements;

---

[1] *Encyclopaedia, Logic,* Introduction, § 13.

[2] Here, as before, I refer to Berkeley's earlier statements.   His later
position approximates closely to that of Hegel, but is never fully
thought out.

since it practically leaves the world, as understood by science, quite unexplained.

Setting aside such inadequate systems, it may be doubted whether more than three main possibilities remain. We may have a monistic system, like that of Parmenides and Spinoza. We may have a monadistic system, like that of Leibniz, or again like that of Plato, which has many points of similarity. Finally, we may have an organic system, like that of Aristotle or Hegel. A few words must now be devoted to the general consideration of each of these.

4. **The Monistic Type.** The general point of view of Monism has never been more impressively set forth than it was among the ancient Greeks by Parmenides, in opposition apparently to the flux of Heraclitus and the dualism of the Pythagoreans. The system of Spinoza is a more modern expression of the same general position, modified of course by the advance of thought and knowledge. The essence of the position is that ultimate reality is to be thought of as one, indivisible, complete in itself—equally balanced in every way, like a sphere, as it was put by Parmenides. In such a conception of systematic completeness thought finds a certain satisfaction; and perhaps it may be said that all real speculative thought starts from some such point of view. Difficulties at once arise, however, when an attempt is made to explain the existence of the finite and particular from the point of view of this absolute one. Parmenides could only give an account [1] of finite existence according to

---

[1] That this account was intended, as Burnet suggests (*Early Greek Philosophy*, pp. 195 *sqq.*), *merely* as a summing up of the erroneous doctrines of others, seems to me incredible.

what he described as 'the way of opinion.' Spinoza's
system, again, has been compared[1] to a lion's den, towards
which the tracks go, but from which they do not return.
Thought is satisfied by the declaration that all finite things
have to be viewed under the form of eternity. The
difficulty is to explain how there ever comes to be any
other point of view than that of eternity, how there can be
even the appearance of finitude and particularity. The
recent system of Mr. Bradley,[2] seems to labour under somewhat similar difficulties. The Absolute with him is thought
of as the completely coherent and self-consistent ; and with
him also it is rather difficult to see how any place is left for
the incomplete, the incoherent, the contradictory, which yet
in some sense exists. He endeavours to get over the
difficulty by the old conception of degrees of truth and
reality.[3] But it is doubtful whether this is a legitimate way
of escape, unless the whole conception of the Absolute
is at the same time modified. The Absolute would seem
from this point of view to be alone the truly real, the
ultimate subject of all predication ; and the fundamental
difficulty would seem to be that it is a subject to which
no predicate can without contradiction be attached.[4]

5. **The Monadistic Type.** The best known system of

---

[1] In Schwegler's *History of Philosophy.*

[2] *Appearance and Reality.*

[3] Reproduced from Medieval Realism. See Windelband's *History of
Philosophy*, § 23, 2. For an account of Hegel's use of this conception,
see Baillie's *Origin and Significance of Hegel's Logic*, especially pp.
361-3. See also A. E. Taylor's *Elements of Metaphysics*, pp. 108 *sqq.*

[4] See on this point the very interesting paper by Mr. Bertrand Russell
in *Mind*, July, 1901, pp. 308-309. Cf. also the same writer's *Philosophy
of Leibniz*, pp. 12 *sqq.*

the Monadistic type is that of Leibniz. This appears at first to be opposed to the system of Spinoza, but has in reality much in common with it. The Absolute, however, from this point of view, is thought of, not as one, but as many independent realities, which yet have a real communion with one another, and have their ultimate explanation in the principle of the good. This point of view is in the end almost identical in its most essential features with that of Plato, with whom the one of Parmenides becomes transformed into a system of absolute ideas or types, having communion with one another, and finding their ultimate explanation in the supreme idea of the good. The chief difficulty of all such systems lies in the artificiality of the relationship between the supreme principle, the idea of the good, and the particular realities which are conceived as having an independent reality. If one insists on the independence of the particular realities, their communion becomes unaccountable. If, on the other hand, one insists on the ultimate unity, it is difficult to avoid falling back upon the one of Parmenides or Spinoza.

6. **The Organic Type.** By the organic type of speculative construction is here meant the attempt to see the world as a real unity of elements having a certain relative independence. It is described as organic, because the unity thus conceived is of the same general nature as that which is ascribed to a living organism. No doubt it may be said that even those systems which are described as monistic or monadistic aimed in reality at such a unity. All speculative constructions may be said to have the same aim, and to have a general family resemblance even in the working of it out. But those that have been characterised as monistic or monadistic seem to fail conspicuously to

realise the conception of organic unity, either through an undue emphasis on the unity of the whole, as against the particular elements which form its content, or by undue emphasis on the independence of certain special modes of reality (whether, as with Plato, ultimate types or ideas, or, as with Leibniz, individual realities).

In the ancient world the best example of a system of the kind that is here described as organic is that of Aristotle. He perceived the difficulties involved in Plato's conception of a world of independent realities distinct from the particular content of experience; and against this he maintained that the world of our experience is a real whole, within which all the particular contents have organic relations. He failed, however, to work out this conception satisfactorily, partly perhaps from the lack of an adequate theory of development. Instead of presenting us with a continuous process, he represents the world as a scale of successive steps; and it is difficult to see how the first and last steps are related to one another. At the one end is the first Matter; at the other is the pure Form of thought. Granting these, it is possible to give a fairly coherent account of the intermediate modes of reality; and probably no one has ever been more successful than Aristotle in bringing the subject matter of experience, so far as known to him, into a coherent and systematic form. But the two ends of the scale seem to lack organic connection.

In modern times it can hardly be doubted that Hegel is the writer who best represents the organic point of view. He is hardly as successful as Aristotle in dealing with the concrete material—partly, it may be, because this is so much more complex in modern times. On the other hand, he is able to give a more satisfactory account of the general connection of the leading elements in his system. This he does by thinking of the universe as a self-differentiating system. The unity of the whole necessarily expresses itself in the growing life of the parts. How far this conception is really capable of being systematically worked out, is obviously a question that cannot be answered in such an elementary work as the present[1]; but we may say that, if any system of philosophy can be made ultimately satisfactory and coherent, one on the general lines of the Hegelian has probably the best chance of meeting the necessary requirements.[2]

7. **The Problem of Evil again.** The significance of these various speculative constructions is perhaps nowhere more apparent than in the ways in which they respectively deal with that fundamental problem of evil, to which reference has already been made. It is the tendency of Monistic systems in general to deny the reality of evil,[3] as of the finite altogether. The result of this is of course to deny the reality of good as well, since this is only intelligible by contrast. Hence in Spinoza's system ethical

---

[1] The most interesting attempt to work it out in recent times is undoubtedly that of Mr. M'Taggart in his *Studies in Hegelian Cosmology*, chap. ix. The attempt does not appear to be entirely successful; but it is impossible to discuss it here.

[2] Hegel himself seems to proceed throughout on the assumption that a coherent speculative construction can be worked out. Perhaps he would say, like Mr. Bradley, that this is one of the 'rules of the game.' But it certainly gives his procedure a certain air of dogmatism. One wants at least to know what place that particular game has in the great playtime of human life. Cf. Baillie's *Origin and Significance of Hegel's Logic*, p. 349.

[3] A similar tendency may be noted in such poetry as that of Walt Whitman.

determinations are not regarded as having any ultimate value.   Yet an ethical ideal is recognised by Spinoza, and a similar inconsistency would seem to appear in most systems of the same type.   Monadistic systems, on the other hand, tend to be more or less Manichean.   With Leibniz this is 'the best of all possible worlds'; but it is not possible to have a world absolutely good, on account of the element of passivity or negation that belongs to the nature of the finite.   But this raises the question, why there should be a finite world at all; and the same question presents itself with regard to the system of Plato, where the finite appears as a falling off from the eternal type of good.   The point of view that connects itself with the third method of construction is that which seeks to show that the differentiation of an organic unity necessarily involves the elements of negation and conflict.   There can be no real unity, it is contended, without differentiation of parts; and this involves the breaking up of the harmony of the whole and its restoration again.   The broken music which arises in this process may, from the point of view of the whole, seem perfect harmony; but for us, who are at the point of view of the parts, there is necessarily something of the nature of evil.   How far such a view can be satisfactorily worked out, it is of course impossible for us here to determine; but it seems clear at least that it is the only view that offers a satisfactory solution, if it can be consistently developed.[1]

8. **Limitations of Speculative Construction.**   The weakness of all speculative construction lies in the fact that

---

[1] For further discussion of the problem of evil, reference may be made to Bradley's *Appearance and Reality*, Book II., chap. xvii.

its ultimate aim does not appear to be completely attainable by man. Its aim is that of enabling us to view experience as a whole, and to see it as a completely coherent, self-consistent, and satisfactory system. This would be in the full sense impossible, unless we could attain to a complete knowledge of the whole. Human knowledge, starting as it does from the point of view of an individual focus, and growing gradually outwards from point to point, does not seem to be capable of any such completeness. It can never yield us more than an ideal outline of the whole. And even such an ideal outline must be to some extent tentative and unsatisfactory, so long as our knowledge of the broad features of the universe remains so incomplete and hypothetical as even the latest advances of science still leave it. Yet a tentative philosophy is almost a contradiction in terms, in view of the peculiar certainty and completeness at which all speculative construction aims. On this particular point Hegel seems to have been guilty of a sophism. In meeting the objection that we can nowhere point to the complete philosophy, he says [1] that it is as if some one were to

---

[1] *Encyclopaedia, Logic*, Introduction, § 13. Of course, if one frankly recognises the tentative character of all philosophic construction, the objection no longer holds. The point is very well put by Mr. Bradley (*Appearance and Reality*, Introduction, p. 6) : "Whether there is progress or not, at all events there is change ; and the changed minds of each generation will require a difference in what has to satisfy their intellect. Hence there seems as much reason for new philosophy as for new poetry. In each case the fresh production is usually much inferior to something already in existence ; and yet it answers a purpose if it appeals more personally to the reader. What is really worse may serve better to promote, in certain respects and in a certain generation, the exercise of our best functions. And that is why, so long as we

object that we can nowhere point to the complete fruit. Pears, cherries, etc., are after all fruit, though they are only particular kinds of fruit, not the final fruit, or fruit as it is in itself. But this answer overlooks the fact (perhaps to some extent concealed by the German idiom) that in dealing with fruit we do not want one final fruit, but only a succession of particular fruits. But a system of philosophy, like a system of geometry or chemistry, aims at supplying us with *the* truth. If it only gives us one among many guesses at truth, or partial approximations to truth, it is not exactly what it aims at being.

9. **Defence of Speculative Construction.** In the foregoing section, I have played the part of *advocatus diaboli* against the claims of a speculative synthesis. It seems necessary now to add something in justification of such attempts. In the cases of the perceptual, the scientific, the aesthetic, and the ethical constructions, it hardly appeared necessary to give any such justification. No one really doubts the validity of perceptual construction or of the constructions contained in our ordinary knowledge ; and even with regard

---

alter, we shall always want, and shall always have, new metaphysics." The only objection to this is that speculative construction seems to aim at being something more than an 'exercise of our best functions.' Philosophy appears in this respect to be more like religion than like poetry. The lover of poetry can enjoy Homer, Aeschylus, Dante, Shakespeare, Goethe, Browning, etc., and is never troubled by the thought that none of them is final. The religious man, on the other hand, is little comforted by knowing that there is Polytheism, Buddhism, Judaism, Christianity—all unquestionably religions—if he may not accept any of them as true. The man who really cares about philosophy has perhaps a similar feeling.

to scientific construction—so long as it remains within its own province—any doubts that are brought forward are rather of the nature of exercises in scepticism than indications of any serious want of confidence. Nor does any one really doubt that it is possible to recognise and to produce something that is truly beautiful, and to do something that is intrinsically praiseworthy. The efforts of religion and philosophy, on account of their larger aims, are more open to question. It is probable, however, that few would really doubt that the attitude of mind expressed by the term religion has a certain value for the human consciousness. Doubt has reference mainly to the objective truth of the view of the world which the religious attitude implies. On this objective side, the contents of the religious and the speculative construction would appear to coincide. Thus it may be said that the speculative construction is the only one about which there is any serious dispute. We have to ask, therefore, what is the justification for this effort of the human mind.

The answer appears to be, primarily, that this effort is really involved in all other efforts after intellectual synthesis. They are all efforts to make our experience into an intelligible system; and speculative construction simply brings the nature of these efforts to clear consciousness. If it be urged, that the result of this clear consciousness is merely to shew that in the end all such efforts stultify themselves, since we see on reflection that no such complete intelligibility is possible; the answer is that this is not a fair statement of the result. It may be allowed that a completely coherent view of the system of experience is not possible for any finite consciousness; but if it can be shewn that it is possible to think of the universe as a whole in a way that is not hopelessly incoherent, something valuable has been accomplished. Now it may be maintained that this is what the great speculative constructions have to some extent done; and, so far as they have really done this, it may be said that they are all justified. The fact that they are all in some respects different is not, from this point of view, a serious objection. For the differences are partly removed when the various systems are cleared of their inconsistencies; and it may be contended that the differences that remain are due largely—if not entirely—to the fact that the writers who constructed them were approaching the subject by different avenues. If different ways of approaching it lead to substantially similar conclusions, this tends to confirm the general result, rather than to throw doubt upon it. In this sense we may maintain that the philosophic systems are all fruits—fruits that have value for their own sakes, and still greater value when they are compared with one another. And this is perhaps what Hegel really had in mind in the passage that was quoted above. A justification of this position, however, could only be arrived at by a detailed consideration of the leading philosophical constructions, and a comparison of their results—a task which is far beyond the limits of our present treatment. But these remarks may at least serve to shew that any limitations that may fairly be recognised in the way of speculative construction are not necessarily fatal to its value.[1]

---

[1] On this subject there are some very instructive remarks in Mr. H. H. Joachim's recent book on *The Ethics of Spinoza*, pp. 99-101. Cf. also Bradley's *Appearances and Reality*, chap. xxvii. The above considerations contain incidentally one of the main justifications for

studying philosophy historically. The comparison of different systems supplies one of the chief tests of the validity of any one system. Another justification for the historical method of study has also been supplied incidentally in the course of this book, by the emphasis that has been laid on the genetic character of human thought. In going through the history of philosophic thought we are studying *the human mind philosophising;* and it is only by watching how it grows that we can judge the value of its results.

CHAPTER VII.

CONCLUSION.

It is not necessary to add much to what has gone before in the way of general summary. We have given some account of the nature and growth of human knowledge, and have indicated the ideal constructions to which it points. We have also seen what are the chief difficulties in the way of carrying out such ideal constructions. A few words may now suffice to bring together the main results of this survey.

Broadly speaking, it may be said that the results of our inquiry might conceivably have appeared in three different forms. The most satisfactory result, at least on a first view,[1] would no doubt have been that of being able to bring out successfully the exact nature of the various constructions that have to be made in each case, and to show that they could be thoroughly carried out

---

[1] When it is remembered that a success of this kind would to a large extent destroy the significance of intellectual effort, its satisfactoriness becomes more open to doubt. Human life seems to be so essentially bound up with imperfection that to introduce perfection at any point would be to kill it. Yet it is equally killed if at any point the effort after perfection fails.

against every imaginable difficulty, so as to give complete satisfaction to the constructive impulses of thought. That our result is not of this triumphant character is perhaps only too painfully apparent. On the other hand, we might have discovered such difficulties in the way as to lead us to distrust entirely the powers of the human mind in the building up of knowledge, either in all its aspects or in some of the most important of them. I would wish to urge that this also is not exactly the result to which we are led. The third possibility is to acknowledge certain serious difficulties in the constitution of human knowledge, but at the same time to recognise indefinite possibilities of gradually removing such difficulties, or at least of reducing them to a minimum. On the whole, it is to a result of this last character that I should wish to point as the conclusion of our inquiry.

I would urge, in the first place, that the general result of our survey cannot be fairly described as a sceptical one, although it is clear that we have had to recognise serious difficulties in the way of knowledge at every point in its construction. The most complete kind of scepticism would seem to be that of the kind that is best represented by the ancient followers of Heraclitus, according to whom even the correct naming of objects is properly speaking impossible. This amounts to saying that even the perceptual construction of things and events is one that cannot be carried out. But scepticism of this kind would, as Aristotle said, reduce us to the condition of vegetables. Even the consciousness of animals is enough to refute it; for even there the apprehension of kinds is at least implicitly present; and the fact that the animals can in some degree work out their lives, shows that this mode of construction has some objective value. This at least suffices to convince us that the world is at any rate not a mere chaos. A less extreme form of scepticism is that which throws doubt on the possibility of scientific construction. This is perhaps best represented by the more modern scepticism of Hume. But this again is sufficiently refuted by the actual growth of the sciences. Kant seems to have been justified in his contention that the actual work of the physical science changes the problem from—Is physical science possible? to How is physical science possible? Many of the speculations of science are highly hypothetical; there are many loose ends in its constructions; but that a large body of knowledge can be built up with genuine objective significance is a truth that is beyond the reach of any sane scepticism. The question remains whether scepticism is more reasonable with regard to those constructions that carry us beyond the sphere of positive science. Here we come upon the various theories with regard to the limitations of human knowledge that are associated with the names of Locke, Kant, the modern Agnostics, etc. Now the general conclusion to which we seem to be led is that this kind of scepticism is essentially the same in kind as the other two, and can only be met in the same way. It is not so easy to meet it, because we cannot point to similarly successful achievements in those constructions that go beyond the range of science. When we ask whether there is any real ground for confidence in our fundamental moral convictions, or in that general view of the rational significance of the universe which is expressed in religion, we are raising larger and more difficult problems than any with which we are confronted in physical science. But on the whole the answer seems to be the same in kind. Great as the difficulties may be in the fundamental problems which these constructions imply, they yet are constructions that are necessary for the working out of certain aspects of our experience; and there seems no real reason for doubting that such constructions also have a genuine objective significance. But it is no doubt true that, the larger the construction is, the more difficult does it become to vindicate it by an appeal to the successful working of it out. Our confidence that fire burns, that a house shelters us, that the sun rises, is continually being vindicated by the common experiences of life. Our confidence in the law of gravitation or the principles of optics is more difficult to make good; and most people may more reasonably doubt them. That history has a rational significance, that the universe is an intelligible whole, are beliefs of a still wider compass; and the experiences that tend to verify them cannot so readily be rounded off and presented as concrete facts. Yet on the whole they are constructions that are equally necessary for the coherence of our experience; and it seems reasonable to regard them with a certain modest confidence.

On the whole, then, I would urge that the broad result of metaphysical inquiry is to lead us to have a general conviction of the reliability of experience as a whole, coupled with a general distrust of the finality of any particular aspect of it.[1] I should hardly care to repeat the

---

[1] The practical value of the philosophies of Aristotle and Hegel seems to me to lie largely in the completeness with which they have brought this out. In other words, it lies in their concreteness. The philosophy of the present time is only very slowly learning to emulate them in this respect.

epigram of Bradley, that this is the best of all possible worlds, and every particular thing in it is a necessary evil; but I would say rather that experience as a whole seems to deserve our fullest trust, though every special element in it, when separated from the whole, is open to the gravest suspicion. What metaphysical inquiry leads us to deprecate, in short, is that sort of fanaticism which sets one aspect of experience against another. The perceptual fanatic trusts only what he can see and handle, and denounces everything farther as idle dreaming. The scientific fanatic believes only in what can be weighed and counted, and ridicules alike the speculator and the man of common sense. The moral fanatic follows his narrow maxims though the heavens fall. The aesthetic fanatic worships a light that leads to swamps and abysses. The religious fanatic has a vision of God that blots out the world and his fellowmen. The metaphysical fanatic is so deeply interested in everything that he cares for nothing. Against all this we have to set the view that experience is an organic whole, in which each part has value only in the light of all the rest. Take any construction by itself, and it fails; take it in relation to the whole, and we may reasonably believe that it does not fail. Perhaps this is a disappointing result; but at any rate to get to any more satisfying haven would require a longer voyage.

It would be a mistake, however, to conclude even an introductory sketch of Metaphysics with what might seem like a despairing note. The truth is that metaphysical inquiry, though it has exercised the mind of man almost from the very dawn of his intelligence, is still only in its initial stages. It is the foundation of all the higher interests of human life, very much in the same way in which mathematics is the foundation of the physical sciences; but it is much more difficult than mathematics, and can perhaps hardly hope ever to be an exact science in quite the same sense. But it is gradually getting into a more systematic shape; and there is every ground for hoping that in a comparatively short time it will offer a much firmer foundation for all those things that lie nearest to the inner heart of man than it can claim to do at present.

NOTE ON METAPHYSICAL LITERATURE.

THE study of Metaphysics, it must be confessed, is rendered specially difficult by the fact that it has not yet emerged from the stage, through which most subjects have had to pass, of being a battle-ground for rival schools of thought. So long as this is true, it is hardly possible to guide the student satisfactorily among the complex issues of the subject. For rival schools tend not only to offer different solutions of the problems, but even to raise the problems in different forms. The conflict is thus apt to appear like a war between two hostile states, of which one elects to fight by land and the other by sea ; so that they hardly ever come into any real contact with one another. There is, however, in metaphysics, as in other subjects, a gradual approximation to unanimity, at least with respect to the way in which the problems ought to be formulated. The student who desires further guidance with regard to the nature of the various problems of metaphysics may be referred to the various introductions to philosophy that have been published in recent years. Those by Külpe, Paulsen and Höffding are perhaps more particularly to be recommended. For the history of the development of speculative thought, the introductory book by Rogers [1] will probably be found most satisfactory ; while for the purpose of more advanced study there is nothing better than the work of Windelband. In addition to these,

---

[1] *A Student's History of Philosophy.*

Burnet's *Early Greek Philosophy* may be mentioned as providing an extremely suggestive introduction to the beginnings of philosophical inquiry ; and Adamson's *Development of Modern Philosophy* as concentrating attention on the latest forms in which the problems of metaphysics are presented.

The works dealing with particular philosophical systems are too numerous to mention. Full information on this point may be found in the bibliography contained in the third volume of Baldwin's *Dictionary of Philosophy and Psychology*. Some of these works, however, are specially noteworthy as having an interest which is not purely historical. Caird's *Critical Philosophy of Kant* is not only a summary and criticism of the whole Kantian position, but also a discussion—on the whole, the most complete and thorough that we possess—of the basis of modern idealism. The two books by Dr. M'Taggart— *Studies in Hegelian Dialectic* and *Studies in Hegelian Cosmology*—are, in like manner, much more than inquiries into the fundamental doctrines of one particular philosopher. Such works as Russell's *Philosophy of Leibniz*, Jones's *Philosophy of Lotze*, Pringle Pattison's *Scottish Philosophy* and *Hegelianism and Personality*, may also be referred to as having considerably more than a purely historical interest.

With regard to the schools of philosophy that prevail at the present time, a few general remarks may be found useful.

A generation or two ago it might have been fairly said—in this country at least—that the dominant type of philosophy was dualistic. Descartes set the fashion in this direction ; and, though it really broke down in the hands of his great followers, Spinoza and Leibniz, it was continued in another form by Reid and Hamilton. Against this there was the materialistic system of Hobbes, which tended for a long time, in a more or less definite way, to dominate the thought of many of the leading representatives of the natural sciences. On the other side, there was the doctrine of subjective idealism, of which the leading representative was Berkeley, and which was carried on, through Hume, into the systems of those who are commonly known as the sensationalists, such as the two Mills, Bain, etc. A reconciliation between materialism and this type of sub- jective idealism was attempted by Herbert Spencer and those others who are usually referred to as Agnostics. All these lines of thought, however, have ceased to be prominently represented among our modern metaphysicians. The prevailing point of view at the present time is a monistic one, and in general with a leaning toward idealism. Quite recently, how- ever, considerable prominence has been given to what is known as Pragmatism, or, more vaguely, as a new Humanism. The primary characteristic of this is its emphasis on the volitional aspect of human experience, as having an importance at least equal to the more purely intellectual aspect. The 'will to believe' has been emphasized in a way that recalls the old Protagorean formula that 'Man is the measure of all things.' The general tendency of this line of thought has been to intro- duce scepticism with regard to the possibility of any ultimate or absolute truth, as distinguished from what we are entitled to affirm as relatively true for us here and now. Pragmatism tends, however, to connect itself with Pluralism—*i.e.* with the affirmation of the separate and independent reality of individual persons. What has been called 'Personal Idealism' is associ- ated with the same point of view.

Still more recently, a point of view commonly described as the 'New Realism' has been, more or less definitely, developed. This may be characterised generally as a new form of Dualism— a form, however, in which the antithesis is not that between mind and matter, but that between consciousness and the objects that are presented to it.

These recent attitudes of Pragmatism and Realism derive their interest largely from their opposition to the current Monism. Pragmatism is especially opposed to any too facile professions of the possibility of knowing the Absolute. Realism, on the other hand, is specially opposed to subjective idealism, and to the tendencies in that direction that are often associated with modern monistic systems.

The modern idealistic position is perhaps most fully and satisfactorily expounded and defended in Caird's *Critical Philosophy of Kant*, to which reference has already been made. Unfortunately, however, it is not always easy to disentangle the more positive and constructive parts of this work from the exposition and criticism of Kant. Bradley's *Appearance and Reality* is written in a more independent and constructive way, and is undoubtedly the most considerable piece of constructive metaphysics in recent times. But it has some very serious defects. It is divided into two parts, one critical and one constructive, and the connexion between these is hardly sufficiently close. It suffers also from a very strong infusion of subjective idealism ; and the use that is made in it of the logical principle of contradiction and of the conception of Degrees of Reality is extremely questionable. Ward's *Naturalism and Agnosticism* is another very important defence of the idealistic position, which is specially valuable on the more critical side. The criticism of the conceptions of the natural sciences contained in this work is probably the most searching to which they have ever been subjected. On the more constructive side it is more sketchy and unsatisfying ; but it is hoped that it will shortly be followed by another work of a more constructive character. It is perhaps, in its present form, especially unsatisfactory in its treatment of volition, in which it shews a certain approximation to the position of Pragmatism. Royce's book on 'The World and the Individual' is extremely original and suggestive ; but the conceptions of Infinity and Freedom on which its constructions mainly rest are open to a good deal of doubt. Professor A. E. Taylor has recently done very valuable work, in his *Elements of Metaphysics*, in the way of bringing together the leading ideas of Bradley, Ward, and Royce, and making clear the ultimate nature of their results. His work rests mainly on that of Bradley. Its exposition is clearer and more coherent than that of Bradley ; but it is doubtful whether in other respects it is free from the fundamental defects of the latter. It is greatly to be regretted that Mr. Taylor has not more fully appreciated the work of Caird. The writings of Dr. M'Taggart, to which reference has already been made, are of great value, especially in determining the way in which the Absolute has to be ultimately conceived ; and Bosanquet's *Logic* may also be referred to as throwing much light upon idealistic epistemology.

On Pragmatism the chief works to which reference should be made are *The Will to Believe* by Professor William James and *Humanism* by Mr. F. C. S. Schiller. The series of essays on *Personal Idealism*, edited by Mr. H. Sturt, should also be consulted[1] ; and many discussions on the subject are to be found in *Mind* and other philosophical journals. The sceptical attitude of Mr. A. J. Balfour, as expressed in his *Defence of Philosophic Doubt* and *Foundations of Belief*, seems to have a very considerable affinity with the point of view of Pragmatism ; and the writings of Professor Pringle Pattison—such as *Man's Place in the Cosmos*—shew some leanings in the same direction.

The new Realism rests perhaps mainly on the writings of Avenarius, a good account of which has recently been given in *Mind* by Mr. Norman Smith. The articles by Mr. G. E. Moore in that journal should also be referred to. Mr. Russell's book on Leibniz and his work on *The Principles of Mathematics* represent the same general stand-point. Mr. Hobhouse's *Theory of Knowledge* and the more constructive parts of Adamson's *Development of Modern Philosophy* may also be taken as representing the tendency towards Realism. The modern realistic position is, however, still only in the making.

For the bearings of Metaphysics on Ethics, the discussions in Caird's *Kant* and Bradley's *Appearance and Reality* should be supplemented by those in Green's *Prolegomena to Ethics* and Taylor's *Problem of Conduct*. Its bearings on Aesthetics are best represented by Bosanquet's *History of Aesthetic* ; and

---

[1] Reference may also be made to Mr. Sturt's more recent work entitled *Idola Theatri*, which is a criticism of some modern idealistic constructions.

on Religion by Caird's *Evolution of Religion*, and by the writings of M'Taggart—especially *Some Dogmas of Religion* and *Studies in Hegelian Cosmology*.

For further light on the literature bearing upon Metaphysics and cognate subjects, Baldwin's *Dictionary of Philosophy and Psychology* should be consulted.

INDEX OF NAMES.